Better Homes and

Kitchen

PLANNER

Better Homes and Gardens® Books
Des Moines, Iowa

Better Homes and Gardens® Books
An imprint of Meredith® Books

Kitchen Planner
Editor: Paula Marshall
Contributing Editors: Cynthia Adams, Lisa Kingsley, Diane Witosky
Contributing Technical Editor: George Granseth
Art Director: Mick Schnepf
Contributing Art Director: David Jordan
Copy Chief: Terri Fredrickson
Managers, Book Production: Pam Kvitne, Marjorie J. Schenkelberg
Contributing Copy Editor: Chardel Blaine
Contributing Proofreaders: Debbie Smith, Willa Speiser, Garland Walton
Contributing Illustrator: The Art Factory
Indexer: Kathleen Poole
Electronic Production Coordinator: Paula Forest
Editorial and Design Assistants: Kaye Chabot, Mary Lee Gavin, Karen Schirm

Meredith® Books
Editor in Chief: James D. Blume
Design Director: Matt Strelecki
Managing Editor: Gregory H. Kayko
Executive Editor, Home Decorating and Design: Denise L. Caringer

Director, Sales, Special Markets: Rita McMullen
Director, Sales, Premiums: Michael A. Peterson
Director, Sales, Retail: Tom Wierzbicki
Director, Book Marketing: Brad Elmitt
Director, Operations: George A. Susral
Director, Production: Douglas M. Johnston

Better Homes and Gardens® **Magazine**
Editor in Chief: Karol DeWulf Nickell
Executive Building Editor: Joan McCloskey

Meredith Publishing Group
President, Publishing Group: Stephen M. Lacy

Meredith Corporation
Chairman and Chief Executive Officer: William T. Kerr

Chairman of the Executive Committee: E. T. Meredith III

All of us at Better Homes and Gardens® Books are dedicated to providing you with information and ideas to enhance your home. We welcome your comments and suggestions. Write to us at: Better Homes and Gardens Books, Home Decorating and Design Editorial Department, 1716 Locust St., Des Moines, IA 50309-3023.

If you would like to purchase any of our home decorating and design, cooking, crafts, gardening, or home improvement books, check wherever quality books are sold. Or visit us at: bhgbooks.com
If you would like to purchase any of our books, check wherever quality books are sold. Visit our website at bhg.com or bhgbooks.com.

Note to the Reader: Due to differing conditions, tools, and individual skills, Meredith Corporation assumes no responsibility for any damages, injuries suffered, or losses incurred as a result of following the information published in this book. Before beginning any project, review the instructions carefully, and if any doubts or questions remain, consult local experts or authorities. Because local codes and regulations vary greatly, you always should check with local authorities to ensure that your project complies with all applicable local codes and regulations. Always read and observe all of the safety precautions provided by any tool or equipment manufacturer, and follow all accepted safety procedures.

Contents

What's 1 in a Kitchen

Loaded with personal expression, today's kitchens are a home's gathering place.

Opposite: This airy kitchen features a relatively new trend—the commercial stove. It also makes good use of an established trend—the center island. With its whimsical art and colorful pottery, this is a warm and highly personal space that's a great place not only to cook, but also simply to gather in to catch up with each other, create more art, or do homework.

You're thinking kitchens! Are your ideas, needs, and wants coming to you in bits and pieces? Whether you're building a new kitchen or reworking an existing one, doing the design work yourself or working with a pro, this book can help pull your dreams together.

This chapter is an appetizer of sorts, a place to start anticipating the process. At this chapter's end, you'll find a kitchen quiz. Your answers will help you sort out your needs and wants, and will bring to light the kind of kitchen that will work for you.

The next chapters will take you through all the options in kitchen layout, materials, and everything else. Mentally try on the ideas presented in these chapters. When you arrive at the final chapter that deals with the nitty gritty of measuring spaces and drawing up plans, you'll be ready—and you'll be ready to turn your dreams into a wonderful new space in your home.

A hand-painted mural on the refrigerator door personalizes and adds a touch of whimsy to this kitchen. Rich color in the forest-green cabinets and in the Turkish-style rug on the sunny wood floor makes a strong design statement.

Make It Your Own

"I ask people, 'What do you like about your home or its contents?' A collection of antiques, for instance, is a nice way to develop a theme in a kitchen; let's create a space to display them. I ask, 'What are you passionate about?' I tell them to go to showrooms and look at gadgets and creature comforts. What color or texture or finish do they like? Create a file of those elements. Do a test drive in someone else's kitchen—make them dinner, or take a cooking class. Maybe that commercial stove is really frivolous." —Architect Patricia O'Neill, AIA

Above: **Collections of any kind, antique or not, give your kitchen a distinct personality that reflects your interests. A wall of checkerboard coffee-and-cream tile is the perfect backdrop for this homeowner's collection of Queen's ware soup tureens.**

Smart Layout

Below: **The classic work triangle of sink, stove, and refrigerator in this kitchen is nearly perfect, with each one situated in the middle of each of the three walls. The remaining wall was knocked out to open the kitchen to the rest of the house.**

"You need an efficient work space that fits your needs. You may have two or three work zones. You might have a prep-and-cleanup zone or a baking station; people with children might have a snack station. You might have a coffee or juice bar." —Interior Designer Shirley McFarlane, CKD

"Work triangles and zones are more important than ever, but that doesn't always have to mean a bigger kitchen. You might have two 5-foot work areas instead of one long one, positioning the fridge and the range with areas on either side." —Interior Designer Ann Patterson, CKD

Although it's compact, this cherry wood galley kitchen is highly functional. Not an inch of space goes to waste. The island houses two side-by-side ovens for cooking dishes at different temperatures or for entertaining large crowds. Tucked between the refrigerator and the sink is a pullout breadboard. Nearly everything is within arm's reach, but the space still feels generous, thanks to the half-wall created by the island that opens up into the family room.

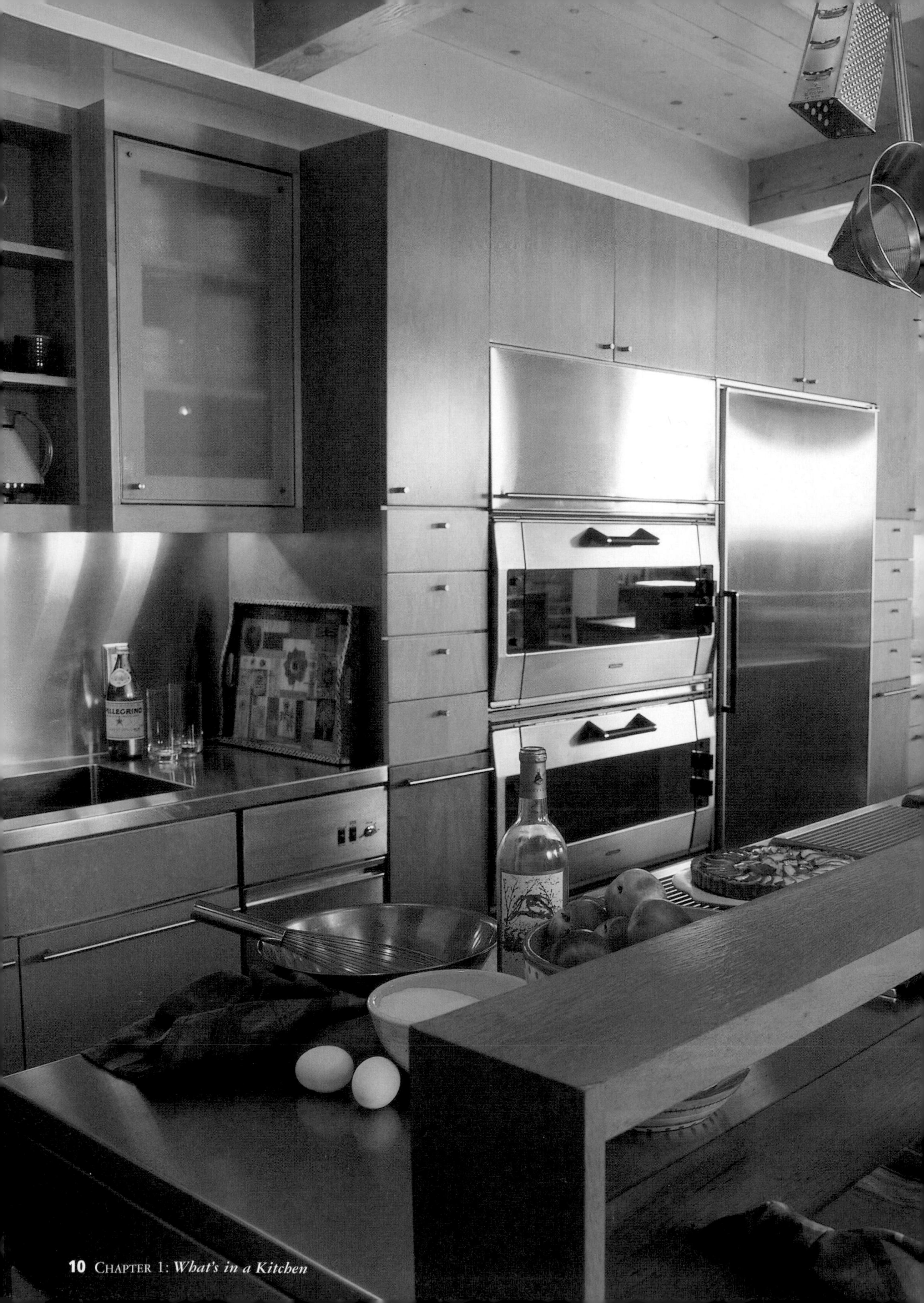

Dual Action

"People are busy now and there are more cooks in the kitchen. People may put in two sinks, one for prep and one for cleanup; or they might put in two refrigerators—or even three—for groceries and snacks. You don't have to go by the book; this is a very personal thing. It's a reorganization of the kitchen."

—Architect Patricia O'Neill, AIA

"Work triangles go hand-in-hand with zoning. Zoning is a big deal. I tell people this is very important when you're preparing oatmeal and he's unloading the dishes."

—Interior Designer Barbara Krier, CKD

Opposite: **The magic number in this professional pastry chef's kitchen is two: Two ovens allow for baking of breads and pastries at different temperatures, and a pair of islands contribute to the overall smooth operation of this kitchen. The large main island contains a sink, a cooktop, and a long ledge for stools; a smaller island is outfitted with a single-bowl round sink, below, and a beverage refrigerator. It serves as a backup work surface. Across from the main island, a third sink and dishwasher separate cleanup from preparation, leaving the serving area free from dirty pots, pans, dishes, and general kitchen clutter.**

Savvy Storage

"People can outgrow their kitchens by not planning; for instance, by not finding a place for the microwave other than on the counter."

—Architect Patricia O'Neill, AIA

"People don't necessarily need to put things away-away. They're using more open shelving, so they have easy access to tools."

—Interior Designer Barbara Brown

"I have people make two lists: a must-have and a would-like-to-have. The recycling and trash, for instance, are things people don't think about. But the trash is something you

Left: Square cutouts in the top three shelves of this lighted pantry allow illumination to reach every shelf; the bottom three shelves pull out.

Below: Baking pans and small appliances that aren't used every day can be easily seen and retrieved when stored in roll-out shelving. Some homeowners install electrical outlets in the back walls of cupboards to allow toasters or coffeemakers to be used on the shelf, then stored out of sight.

have to deal with every day. Are you going to walk across the room to the pantry? Another thing I ask is, 'How many sets of dishes do you have? Which ones do you use every day?'"

— Interior Designer Barbara Krier, CK

Adjoining Rooms

Opposite: When designing a kitchen with an adjoining room, the degree of openness you create between the rooms can vary dramatically. Here, a half-wall and two columns create a sense of separateness between the kitchen and living room but preserve the basic open floor plan.
Below: Weathered wood posts and beams create a frame but no obstruction to the family room.

"Many people want to have a great-room—a family room—as part of the kitchen, or at least adjacent to it, so that the kitchen and family room is one space. People like to have mudrooms and laundry rooms adjacent to the kitchen. People want this kitchen to feel furnished, maybe incorporate a fireplace, or continue the wood floor into it. Some people like a bit of separation, but generally people like their rooms physically and visually connected."—Architect Patricia O'Neill, AIA

"People want to be together when they're home; the great-room concept is still valid. People want laundry stuff near the kitchen. People want to take care of multiple chores when they have a few hours and they don't want to leave family."—Interior Designer Ann Patterson, CKD

Open Kitchen

Opposite: A center island with a narrow base makes the traffic flow around this kitchen smooth and easy. While it functions as a work surface, the island is also pretty and comfortable enough to serve a family three meals a day—and to entertain dinner guests, too, if the cook wants to forgo the formality of sitting in the dining room. Many islands can be put on wheels, so the work/dining space can be moved, and the kitchen can be opened up.

"More and more people would rather have a family dining room in the kitchen to the point of giving up the formal dining room. The kitchen is now a beautiful room with beautiful dining tables.... During the week, people prepare meals that are quick, easy, and served in shifts. But weekends are dedicated to family and friends and entertaining. The kitchen becomes a gracious, relaxed family area."—

Architect Patricia O'Neill, AIA

"There is still a trend away from the dining room. Kitchen tables are growing up."

—Interior Designer Ann Patterson, CKD

HANG ON TO YOUR IDEAS

Now's the time to start a kitchen file. A three-ring binder with folder pockets and see-through zippered envelopes is ideal for stashing notes, brochures, color swatches, and photos pulled from magazines. When you see things you like in magazines, rip them out. Remember exactly what you like by scribbling a note right on the photo. As you gather more and more pictures, recurring themes of what you like will bubble to the surface.

Home Work

"I see people incorporating an area where there's a computer—not an office space, but an information space—where they can leave messages. They're wired and ready to go; it's an extension of the telephone and tackboard, where they can plan meals and order groceries online."—Architect Patricia O'Neill, AIA

"I try to set up a computer; I don't like them obvious, but it's nice to have a computer in the kitchen—maybe it's just a place to plug in a laptop. I suggest this to most people, off to the side. The kids are within earshot; you can see what they're watching or doing or talking about. It's the great-room effect."
—Interior Designer Barbara Krier, CKD

Opposite: This kitchen was fitted with a computer-free desk that matches the rest of the cabinetry. It's a good place for paying bills or making a grocery list.The square footage committed to desk space in the kitchen can vary according to your needs. Below: Space for an Internet-connected computer was tucked into a tiny corner of this kitchen.

Mixed Materials

Opposite: **Combining materials in a kitchen to meet aesthetic and practical considerations is a little like cooking itself: a pinch of this, a pinch of that; it all adds up to a beautiful result. This kitchen uses three different woods plus stainless steel, copper, and granite. The variation in the wood tones adds warmth and visual interest; the stainless is durable and easy to clean, while the copper, cut with decorative motifs, adds a European flair. The granite is beautiful and makes a cool, nonstick surface for rolling out bread, cookie, and pastry dough.**

"People are mixing materials, such as wood cabinets with painted pieces, or mixing different countertops: stone in one, wood in another, stainless steel in another. For an evolved look, this helps the budget, too. You can splurge on one aspect and conserve on another."—Architect Patricia O'Neill, AIA

"Stainless has been with us and will be; certainly, though, we'll see more mixed metals—bronze, zinc, titanium, and lots of copper—some aged. Natural materials are big now and will be in the future."

—Interior Designer Shirley McFarlane, CKD

Furniture Style

"The kitchens of today are more furnished than they have been in the past. We're looking at cabinets as furniture, creating display areas, and adding furniturelike features to cabinets, such as crown molding and pilasters. We're bumping them out, recessing them, making them more interesting. The kitchen is made up of pieces rather than sets." —Architect Patricia O'Neill, AIA

Right: Kitchen cabinets are really just fine furniture that you happen to hang on your wall. As such, these custom-made maple cabinets were built with decorative, furniturelike details such as crown molding, lighted display windows, and a crest above the pass-through. A three-stage paint treatment with a glazed finish was designed to make them appear as if they've aged over time. Unquestionably, though, the tomato-red center island is the focal point of the kitchen. Glass-front storage bins hold colorful grains and pastas in 1-inch-deep display compartments. Distressing the piece allowed the mustard-color paint to glow through several coats of red paint. With its sink and dishwasher, the island functions as the main food-preparation area—but it's also a great place to pull up a chair and make a grocery list, linger over a cookbook, or have coffee with a friend.

Kitchen Quiz

What's in your kitchen?

Ask yourself the following questions and you'll get a better picture of what you already have, what you need, and what you want from your kitchen. If the kitchen is used equally by your spouse or partner, answer the questions together.

■ How much time do you spend in your kitchen?

■ What are you doing when you're there? Are you eating meals, reading, relaxing, or working on projects? Do you use the phone or computer there?

■ Who's in the kitchen with you? Children, friends, family, or colleagues?

■ How does your kitchen make you feel when you're in it? How would you like it to make you feel?

■ If you wrote "A Day in the Life of My Kitchen," how would it read? What's being done in the kitchen and who's there? Would this page be different on weekends or holidays? Would it be different three to five years from now?

■ Do you cook alone or with others? If you cook with others, how many will be sharing the space?

■ What do you cook? Elaborate, all-day dishes or simple, quick meals?

■ How many people do you regularly cook for? How often do you cook for a different number of people?

■ Do you have special cooking interests, such as baking or grilling?

■ What large and small appliances do you use? Are they sufficient? Any special storage needs?

■ What appliances do you use simultaneously?

■ Do you have plenty of work space for your kitchen activities? Is this workspace where you'd like it?

■ Is your storage space for equipment and ingredients adequate and in a place that works for you? Can you find your equipment and ingredients easily?

■ Is your kitchen comfortable for you to work in? Why or why not?

■ Does your kitchen's arrangement cause you physical strain? What adjustments would be most helpful?

■ Does your kitchen work well for everyone who uses it? Do you have any children or other family members with specific height or other needs?

What's in place?

In almost every kitchen begging for a new look, there is an asset or two waiting to be appreciated. Let this question simmer a few days as you discover the best assets of your kitchen space. Do you have a high ceiling or a roomy floor plan? Do you have access to a great view, even if it's limited by a tiny window or none at all? Are your appliances in good shape? Do you have spaces, such as closets or small rooms, near the kitchen that are underused? Your answers may present opportunities for your kitchen that you'd never dreamed possible.

What's your style?

Your personal style may be consistent from your choice of clothing to the decoration of your home, or it may vary widely or with your mood. Whether your style is traditional, contemporary, country, retro, artistic, reflective of a favorite vacation spot—or an eclectic mix of these—remember that you'll be spending time in your kitchen every day. How much time do you want to spend cleaning or maintaining the space? Do you like an uncluttered look, or do you like to have your kitchen stuff out and around you?

Above: Even the smallest kitchens can be fabulous. This condominium kitchen lacks an outside wall, but placing the sink in front of the pass-through mimics the standard sink-under-window configuration found in houses. Well-placed lighting fixtures, light-tone wood cabinets and flooring, and simple features all work to keep the look open. And, with a nod to Yankee ingenuity, by putting one chair on each side, the tiny, narrow peninsula becomes the perfect breakfast nook.

Exploring Your Options

From putting new paint on the walls to tearing them down, the degrees of redo are nearly limitless.

Opposite: **The exposed ductwork and high-tech materials in this loft kitchen exemplify modern style; the openness and physical connection to adjoining living space exemplifies the desire of many modern homeowners for a kitchen that connects in some way to the rest of the home— whatever its style.**

Any kitchen can be completely remade, of course. But there are myriad ways to achieve an inspiring, functional kitchen whether you opt to gut your existing one or not. Take into account the positive aspects of your present kitchen, along with your budget and plans for staying in the house. As you peruse ideas, think about the feasibility of the following routes to your dream kitchen:

■ Refreshing the space with new lighting, hardware, paint or wallcovering, flooring, and furnishings.

■ Boosting the capacity and capability of storage space, electrical and plumbing service, or major appliances.

■ Repairing or replacing elements that are worn or defective.

■ Rearranging existing space by adding or removing walls, windows, and doors.

■ Claiming or reworking adjacent space.

■ Building an addition.

■ Moving the kitchen's placement in your home's floor plan.

Whatever the boons and banes of your present kitchen, it can be made more efficient and pleasant. As you read on, think about your specific situation and about the possibilities for your own space.

Large kitchens

A large kitchen offers lots of options in terms of design because of its sheer size, but its elements must be arranged carefully to make the space both efficient and comfortable. Generally, a large kitchen should be divided into zones with distinct functions—cooking, eating, and relaxation or play areas—so that each one feels intimate and cozy while remaining a part of the whole.

One of the best ways to accomplish this is with a center island. A cooktop or sink can be built into the island, along with ample counterspace, so that the cook is able to interact with family members in the kitchen rather than face a blank wall. Islands concentrate food preparation, serving, and cleanup zones in one area so the cook doesn't waste time trudging back and forth across a large room with milk jugs, heads of lettuce, knives, cans, or bottles in hand.

Small kitchens

If you live with a small kitchen, you may not be able to outfit it with a fireplace, sofa, art easel, and computer station, but you can

Below: The addition of a banquette breakfast area turned this once-isolated kitchen into a sun-filled and inviting living space.

large kitchen

small kitchen

have a highly efficient and attractive space. What are your minimum kitchen needs? Think about a stove, sink, refrigerator, and food prep/cleanup area. Decide the minimum dimensions within which you can work, then arrange all the necessities—including storage—in that space.

You might also consider if you can take advantage of any adjoining spaces. Can you combine your kitchen with an adjacent room to make a multipurpose cooking/dining/family room? Can you open up a wall, or a half-wall, between your kitchen and the adjoining room to improve flow and increase the sense of space?

Efficient kitchens

It goes without saying that you want your kitchen to be efficient. But you want it to be beautiful, too. The two are not mutually exclusive. Details such as crown molding, bold color choices, or interesting materials can make even the most hard-working kitchen both fun and functional.

efficient kitchen

unfitted kitchen

Above: **Rather than running an unbroken line of cabinets from wall to wall, this unfitted kitchen features a decorative medallion of ceramic tile that, in lieu of a window, gives the cleanup crew something pretty to look at.**

Unfitted kitchens

An idea that came into being in the 1980s is now a full-blown trend that's likely here to stay. The unfitted kitchen features freestanding, furniturelike cabinetry, often paired with hand-crafted or repurposed flea-market finds, to create an eclectic, highly personal look. Unfitted kitchens employ a mix of materials, colors, and shapes and may incorporate work spaces of different heights and materials according to their function. There may be a marble slab for pastry-making, heat-resistant granite near the oven, and a butcher block for chopping and slicing. Pieces of the unfitted kitchen can often be approached from more than one direction, as opposed to a built-in or fitted kitchen, where elements are attached to the walls all the way around the room.

Fitted kitchens

Fitted kitchens came into vogue in the 1950s when matching, streamlined cabinets ran wall to wall. The design is somewhat formal and allows for maximum storage and counter space. Fitted kitchens usually employ standard built-in cabinets, which are more economical than custom cabinets. With a bit of creativity they can have warmth and personality that avoids the pitfall of seeming monotonous or institutional. Put glass fronts on some of the cabinets and light the interiors; use an interesting and functional countertop material; paint the cabinets a bright color; or hire a carpenter to customize one section—perhaps to build open shelving or a dresser for displaying a collection of favorite dishes.

Eat-in kitchens

Even if space is at a premium, try to have an eating area in your kitchen. Party guests and family members seem to congregate there, and you'll have a place for them to sit. This can be accomplished on an island or in a space-saving built-in banquette or window seat. Round tables fit better into small spaces than rectangular or square ones. A small round table (about 4 feet in diameter) will comfortably seat four.

eat-in kitchen

fitted kitchen

Above: A casual kitchen eating area near a window provides a beautiful view any time of the year. Round tables such as this one fit better in small spaces than do square or rectangular tables. A table about 4 feet in diameter will comfortably seat four.
Left: In a small space, a fitted kitchen such as this one with its unbroken banks of cabinetry maximizes both storage space and work space. Visual interest was added to this kitchen with a collection of baskets placed atop the wall cabinets, artfully lit by recessed lighting.

Design
Space

Your kitchen's layout is critical to how much you'll enjoy being in it. Sure, you can fill it with gleaming cabinetry, granite counters, and exotic flooring, but how much will you enjoy the space if you're constantly tripping over children, guests, the dog, or the other cook? The floor plan that will work best for your kitchen will be based on two things: work triangles and zones, and the layouts that are workable in your space.

Building blocks

The kitchen work triangle is formed by the refrigerator, the sink, and the cooktop or range. A line drawn from the center of the sink to the center of the fridge to the center of the cooktop, then back to the sink's center should measure no more than 26 feet. Very active cooks may prefer a triangle of 22 feet or less. In either case, each side of the triangle should measure at least 4 feet but no more than 9 feet.

Zones, also known as work centers, are complementary planning ideas to work triangles. By planning zones for your kitchen and using the triangle concept, you'll ensure that different functions, such as preping,

cooking, and cleaning up, can be carried out without needless collisions. Certainly these chores are likely to occur within a triangle arrangement; other functions are placed outside it. A zone for unloading groceries, for example, requires a stretch of counter space near the refrigerator. A coffee zone with brewer, mugs, spoons, sugar, and cream could be near the sink (or have its own), and be placed where family and guests can help themselves without crossing a cook's path.

Depending on the dimensions of your kitchen, one or more of several basic kitchen shapes will be most efficient and pleasing to you. The basic shapes are, however, just a starting point. Create your kitchen by customizing the basics: Put two shapes together or carve out a 90-degree corner for an angled stretch of counter—whatever you need to get a kitchen that works for you.

■ One-wall kitchens are an efficient use of small, open spaces, but they're not terribly efficient for the cook. They work best with the sink in the center, flanked by fridge and cooktop with 4 feet of counter space between each pair. Place doors away from the one-wall shape to avoid foot-traffic hassles.

More zone ideas:
- Meal planning
- Communications
- Grocery unloading
- Baking
- Snack
- Coffee/Tea
- Recycling
- Baking
- Juicemaking

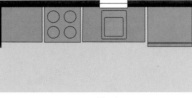

One-wall kitchen

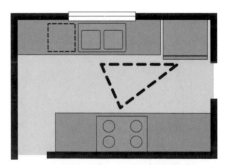

Galley kitchen

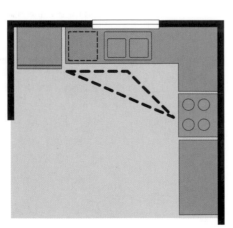

L-shape kitchen

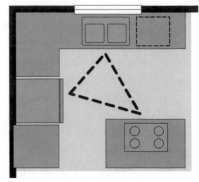

L-shape with island

■ Galley kitchens are built between parallel walls, allowing the cook to move easily from one work area to another. Plan for at least 4 feet of space between opposite counters; think about putting the sink and fridge on one wall with the cooktop centered between them on the opposite wall. If there are doorways at each end of the galley, foot traffic can cross the work triangle.

■ L-shape kitchens require two adjacent walls and are particularly efficient when work areas are kept close to the crook of the L. You'll save yourself extra steps by planning the work flow from fridge to sink to cooking, then to serving areas. Crossing foot traffic is rarely a problem for a cook in the L-shape kitchen.

■ L-shape-with-island kitchens make room for multiple cooks, snack bars, and increased space for storage and family dining. The island also works as a visual room divider.

■ U-shape kitchens usually place one workstation on each of three walls. The design possibilities are many and can be efficient for one cook, but you'll need at least an 8×8-foot kitchen space. Small U-shapes can be a tight squeeze for multiple cooks.

■ U-shape-with-island kitchens solve the dilemma of making a big kitchen efficient. You can work a sink or cooktop into the island, even a special-function countertop such as butcher block for chopping or marble for rolling out pastry. Allow 42 inches of aisle space on all sides of the island; 48 inches is better in a two-cook kitchen.

■ G-shape kitchens feature an island anchored to a line of cabinets. Cooktops or sinks work well situated on the peninsula, which can also function as a dining bar or buffet. The peninsula can be a room divider, allowing family and friends to hang out with the cook without crossing paths.

■ Two-cook kitchens call for work zones or triangles that allow each cook to work without crossing the other's path. Two work triangles can, however, share a leg and are often anchored at the fridge. Multiple-cook arrangements may—but need not— include an extra prep sink, an additional stretch of countertop, or a small second refrigerator.

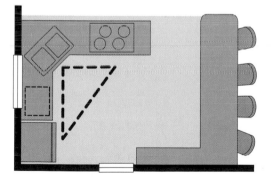

G-shape kitchen

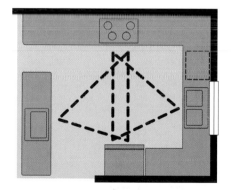

Two-cook kitchen

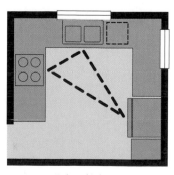

U-shape kitchen

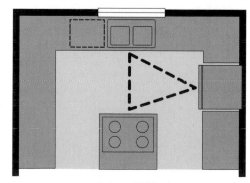

U-shape with island

Rearranging

The average kitchen design remains functional and aesthetically pleasing for about 15 years. That means if you've recently moved into anything but a brand-new house, or have been in your house for even a few years, you're probably itching for a change in your kitchen.

Samespace, new place

Maybe you want to reconfigure your appliances to do away with gridlock around the snack cabinet, microwave, or refrigerator. Maybe you've got a burn mark on your laminate countertop from that big pot of refried beans or beef stew you set down on it, and the blemish has inspired you to start anew. Maybe you simply want a new look. The allure of state-of-the-art appliances, newly available materials for cabinetry, flooring, and countertops, and the latest array of fresh, new colors is undeniable.

One way to design a new kitchen is to stay within the walls of your original kitchen but rearrange its elements. Maybe that's simply a matter of relocating the cabinetry, stove, sink, and refrigerator. Maybe it means adding or removing walls, or adding or enlarging windows and doors. Perhaps a wall can be made into a half-wall to open up the kitchen into an adjacent living area, increasing the sense of space without completely moving any walls at all.

Right: When the 165-square-foot kitchen in this 1920s cottage was redone, the footprint of the room stayed the same as the original kitchen. Every square inch was put to good use. For instance, the corner between the range and sink might have gone unused. Instead, a 3-inch-thick butcher block for chopping vegetables was installed. It features an undercounter bin for compost-ready kitchen scraps with a drawer that tilts out.

Below right: A small peninsula that pokes out between banks of cabinets provides a perfect place for casual dining.

MEASURE TWICE, CUT ONCE

If you must stay within the footprint of your current kitchen, there's an easy way to move around the major players until you get everything to your liking. Plot the shape of your room on graph paper. Sketch in where there are (or where you'd like) windows and doors. Do the same for water pipes, electrical outlets, and heating/cooling vents. Make to-scale cutouts of the appliances you're planning to buy. Move them around your drawing. You might need to buy a smaller appliance or try a different configuration. Sketch in cabinetry and countertops.

The layout of your kitchen is determined by where the four major elements—the sink, range, refrigerator, and dishwasher—are placed. The style of your kitchen can, but certainly doesn't have to, influence its layout. A similarly sized Craftsman-style kitchen and a Mediterranean-style kitchen may each have the stove, sink, refrigerator, and dishwasher in the same spots, but they may be housed quite differently, and the furnishings and materials used may differ greatly. Very contemporary kitchens, often feature banks of streamlined cabinets and are built with high-tech materials.

Left: The long walls of the small kitchen were used for cabinet storage. A mix of several types of cabinets—sage green laminate, honey maple, open shelves, and wood with frosted-glass doors— were used for both eye appeal and budget reasons. Open shelves hold collections and often-used items such as salt and pepper shakers. The microwave oven also has a home on the wall, freeing up valuable counter space.

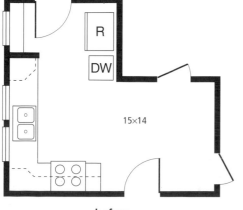

before

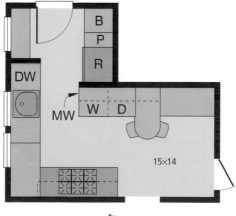

after

Above: If a formal dining room, three-season porch, or mudroom isn't being used to its full potential, space can be annexed from it for an eating area—as it was in this cheery kitchen. A hardworking peninsula divides the cooking space from the eating space while maintaining openness between the two areas.

Reshaping

No matter the shape of your kitchen, more space—for eating, homework, or hanging out—and more efficiency in meal preparation and cleanup are the primary considerations in redesigning today's kitchens.

There are many ways to reshape a kitchen to increase both its space and its efficiency. You can stay within the exterior walls of your house but rearrange the interior walls to meet that goal. Can you annex all or part of an expendable powder room, mudroom, stairwell, or even a formal dining area that is rarely used?

If not, can you knock down the wall that joins the kitchen and an adjoining living area and add an L-shape island where the walls once stood?

There are myriad ways to reshape the kitchen and connect it visually and physically to the main living areas of the house and still keep the rooms separate enough so you don't have your dirty dishes on view. Consider opening the kitchen up to the second floor; or build a half-wall or pass-through so full dishes, empty dishes, and conversation can be passed back and forth between the rooms. Floor or wall cabinets can take the place of floor-to-ceiling walls, islands, or peninsulas as a way to reconfigure your kitchen and open it up.

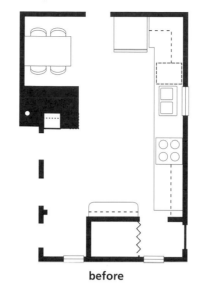

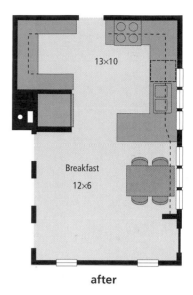

before

after

13×10

Breakfast
12×6

Above, left: An old butler's pantry was turned into a practical and pretty place for storing dishes and displaying art.

Left: Smart layout in this kitchen redo meant that the working spaces—the cooking area and the dining area—were placed on one side of the room, leaving a generous swath for traffic coming into the house from outside and heading for the living room and other parts of the house.

Adding On

These days, it seems everyone wants a bigger kitchen. People aren't just preparing food and eating in kitchens any more. Today's kitchens see all sorts of action—homework, finger painting, paying bills, surfing the Internet, having coffee with a friend.

In new construction, nearly all kitchens are built with ample square footage and are designed to be eating and gathering spaces, with an open connection to at least one other room. But if you have an older house, space constraints can be a real problem.

Unless you're starting from scratch with a brand-new house, adding on—whether it's as simple as a bay window with banquette seating or as complex as a conservatory or an

Above: A computer desk that looks out of a window is a great place to do correspondence, plan menus, or surf the Internet for great recipes.

Right: This is a kitchen for a serious cook who wants friends and family around while preparing dinner. An addition created adequate space for a six-burner professional range— with room to spare.

entire breakfast room—is undoubtedly the ideal (but, alas, most expensive) way to get your dream kitchen.

Start with what you've got

The simplest way to put an addition on your kitchen is to annex or close in an adjoining outdoor space such as a breezeway or porch. Lacking that kind of space, you'll have to build out into your yard. (If you have a two-story house and if your nerves and budget can afford it—and if there is the need—consider building a two-story addition to your house to gain an additional bathroom, office, or bedroom in the process.)

If possible, when you put an addition on your kitchen, design the space so that it opens up to the outdoors. Almost any room in a house benefits from fresh air and sunlight, but perhaps a kitchen does most of all. There are cooking smells to diffuse, and it's where you shuffle in first thing in the morning to wake up, greet the sun, and sip your first cup of coffee of the day. Putting on an addition also gives you the opportunity to add more windows, perhaps in the form of French doors that open out onto a patio.

With access to the outdoors from the kitchen, there are easy-to-reach countertops when you're lugging in groceries. It's also a short trip to and from the garden for picking fresh vegetables and for carrying full plates of food outside for an alfresco dinner on the patio or deck.

Above: **A sizable addition to this house meant that everything—and everyone—could be in the kitchen together: the cook, cookbooks, a beautiful and generous casual dining area, and a comfortable space for hanging out and chatting with the cook.**

There are a few practical matters to consider when planning an addition to a kitchen. You obviously want the addition to blend as seamlessly as possible with the rest of your house (and so do the neighbors). Here are a few pointers for getting the best results out of a renovation:

■ Take careful measurements, do a structural analysis, and give weight to the findings. If you need to upgrade some of the home's underpinnings, spend the money before adding the finishes.

■ Choose materials that combine well with or mimic the home's original palette.

■ Follow your property's dictates. Consider which direction the bulk of the expansion should go. Be sure to look into current building codes. You may need to get an exception or variance from the city before proceeding with your building project.

Even a little space can make a big difference. Here are a few tips for getting the most from a small addition:

■ Consider the angles. An angled addition can provide extra space and run parallel to your property line without looking bulky from the outside.

■ Turn the corners. Wrap an addition around the kitchen, encompassing and enlarging it.

■ Eliminate unneeded doorways to make space for an uninterrupted run of cabinets.

■ Create long sight lines. Plan for unobstructed views from one end of kitchen to the other.

Opposite: There is no shortage of storage space in this newly amended kitchen. A combination of glass-door cabinets, open shelving, and a bank of generously sized drawers provide space for edibles, kitchen gadgets, and several sets of dishware. It does all of this with terrific style that's in keeping with the period and architectural style of the house.

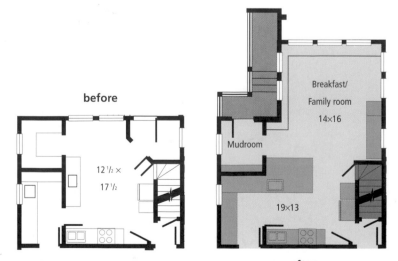

before

12 ½ × 17 ½

after

Breakfast/ Family room 14×16

Mudroom

19×13

Take Your Picks

Get familiar with the newest kitchen materials and most up-to-date appliances before you go shopping.

Opposite: This lovely European-style kitchen reflects many of the current trends in kitchen design: a mix of countertop materials for different uses; the renaissance of linoleum; a large, commercial-style range; and a furnished look that includes an upholstered side chair for kicking back and chatting with the cook.

Whether you're a browser or a serious shopper, a foray to a home improvement center or kitchen and bath store can be exciting, interesting—and mind-boggling. The number of choices in materials, appliances, and accessories for kitchen renovation can be overwhelming. Do you go with stock cabinets or custom-made? Is a granite countertop worth the price tag? Will you really fully use that great-looking commercial range?

Here are the answers to questions about the primary elements in the kitchen: a brief description, price range, and the advantages and drawbacks of the vast array of cabinets, hardware, countertops, backsplashes, flooring, sinks and faucets, lighting, windows, and major appliances on the market today.

Consider how long you intend to stay in your house as you make your choices. If a move is likely to happen in the not-so-distant future, the wiser decision might be not splurging on a dream kitchen but rather taking the practical approach and simply making the current kitchen more functional and a bit more stylish.

Design
Elements

Cabinetry

Probably more than any other element, cabinetry sets the look and feel of your kitchen, and your choices help make it efficient and easy to use. A kitchen remodeler once remarked that cabinets are "basically furniture you hang on your walls." Not surprisingly, their price tag reflects that forthright interpretation.

According to the National Kitchen and Bath Association, nearly half—48 percent— of the average kitchen remodeling budget goes for cabinets. If you choose custom-made cabinets, solid maple or oak, or exotic veneers, don't be surprised if those beauties consume an even bigger piece of the remodeling pie. Accessories, modifications, and unusual finishes increase the costs further.

Below: Some kitchens can incorporate a wall of floor-to-ceiling cabinets that offers unparalleled storage space where you need it most. For convenience in this sort of arrangement, appliances and dishes that are used infrequently should be stored at the very top.

Left: These Dijon-yellow custom cabinets feature traditional recessed panels as well as some beaded-board side panels for a vintage look. Divided-light glass doors offer opportunities to display collections and dishware, as does a built-in plate rack above the big farm-style porcelain sink. Glass-front drawers, grape-and-leaf molding, and turned legs give the island the look of fine old furniture.

Above: Own several sets of dishes? Don't hide them behind closed doors. Cabinets with lots of glass doors provide a great way to display all your pretty tableware. Be sure to install adequate in-cabinet lighting for a beautiful glow at night.

Opposite: Cabinet doors can be embellished with materials other than wood, such as these metal mesh panels. Other options include contrasting wood panels, frosted glass, or metals such as copper.

Depending on how they're constructed and how much they can be customized, cabinets fall into three basic categories: stock cabinets, semicustom cabinets, and custom cabinets.

The category of a particular cabinet is not necessarily an indication of quality; there is fine cabinetry to be had in all three. Look for a blue and white "certified cabinet" seal from the Kitchen Cabinet Manufacturer's Association affixed to any manufactured cabinet, which indicates that it has met certain guidelines

for durable construction. Following is a rundown of the types of cabinets that are currently available and the most common materials from which they're made.

Stock cabinets

Widths for stock cabinets run between 9 and 48 inches, increasing in 3-inch increments. Stock cabinets come in a great number of styles. They can be ordered through retailers, such as home improvement and kitchen and bath centers, and from manufacturers' catalogs. Stock cabinets cost between $50 and $200 per linear foot.

Pros: Stock cabinets are usually the most economical choice. Because they are stored in manufacturer's warehouses, they are also readily available—usually within a week or so of being ordered.

Cons: Because those same cabinets are already built—sitting in a warehouse waiting to be purchased—they also don't come in special sizes. Filler strips can be used to close gaps between a cabinet and an appliance or wall, but that's pretty much the extent to which they can be customized. If only the "real thing"—solid wood—will do for you, it's unlikely you'll find what you're looking for in stock cabinets.

Semicustom cabinets

These cabinets are built only after an order is final. They come in a wider range of styles, construction materials, and colors than stock cabinets. They can be amended easily with storage units and accessories such as pullout bins and lazy Susans. Semicustom cabinets usually run between $150 and $400 per linear foot.

Pros: Because they are constructed after you've placed your order, modifications to standard cabinet sizes can be made. Semicustom cabinets offer a broad selection of finishes and varying cabinet depths that

will give your kitchen a more personal look.

Cons: The primary disadvantage of semicustom cabinets is their higher price tag. They also may take a month or longer to be delivered after they're ordered, but when you're talking about a kitchen that should last up to 15 years, the wait shouldn't be a major issue.

Custom cabinets

These cabinets are built, usually by a local cabinetmaker, from the specific material you choose (usually a hardwood such as maple, cherry, walnut, or oak), in the size, shape, and configuration you choose and with whatever finish you choose. Custom cabinets usually cost between $250 and $1,000 per linear foot.

Pros: The advantages of this choice are obvious: Within the limits of sound construction, your kitchen cabinets can look and function exactly the way you want them to. If you have an oddly shaped kitchen, a curved wall, or some other uniquely interesting aspect to your kitchen, it can be perfectly fitted with custom cabinets. You can, for instance, create a long cabinet without interior partitions to accommodate cookie

Above: When planning your kitchen, be sure to design in enough storage. This essentially fitted kitchen, with its rows of maple cabinetry, has no shortage of cabinet space. An unattached glass-door display cabinet gives the kitchen just a touch of the furnished, unfitted look that is a much-sought-after style these days.

Cons: Far and away, the biggest downside of custom cabinets is their expense. And you can't be in a hurry to get cooking in your kitchen again. True custom-made cabinets take at least 10 weeks—and often longer than that—to complete.

Materials

Wood: Unless you're hiring a custom cabinetmaker, you may have a hard time finding solid wood cabinets. That's OK; many high-quality units are made of plywood or particleboard. Drawer construction is an indication of quality: Look for metal glides with ball-bearing rollers and dovetail assembly or screws and dowels (not staples and glue). Fully extended, the drawer should not wobble from side to side. Be sure the wood grain on doors matches the frame. To shave costs, order paint-grade units and do your own painting.

Laminate: Laminate cabinets are durable and easy to clean and they come in an array of colors. High-pressure laminates perform best but are expensive. For strength, laminate should be applied to the back of doors as well as the front.

Above: Leaving the space above base cabinets free of wall cabinets makes a small kitchen seem bigger and airier—and leaves you free to decorate with items that personalize your kitchen, such as these plate racks and pottery. Hidden hardware on these cabinets contributes to the clean, open look of the kitchen.

Right: Who says kitchen cabinets have to be monotonous? The current trend toward mixing materials in the kitchen extends to the cabinetry. These wall and base cabinets have different finishes. They contribute to the visual interest of the kitchen and make it appear as though it has evolved over time.

trays and roasting pans. If you use an experienced and artful cabinetmaker with a good reputation, the quality of your cabinets will be unsurpassed. Ask to see examples of past work and be sure to ask for references—and check them.

Hardware

If cabinets are furniture you happen to hang on your walls, hardware is jewelry, if you will, on a well-dressed unit. Of course, hardware is also hardworking and has a very important function, and that should be your first consideration when purchasing it. Will that small, sleek, round brass knob work flawlessly on a floor-to-ceiling roll-out pantry loaded with canned goods? Probably not. But a sturdier handle would. One innovative homeowner fitted the drawers holding his heavy cookware with the kind of bowed handle found on hospital doors. After determining if the hardware you love will function well in your kitchen, you can move on to form.

Certain styles of knobs, hinges, and drawer pulls are associated with certain architectural styles or historic periods, but you don't have to be locked into those if you fancy something entirely different. Hardware is one way to personalize and decorate your kitchen.

Selection varies from one cabinetmaker to another. Pricier models usually offer the most sophisticated selections, including decorator-style pulls and hinges made of solid brass or nickel. Despite its name, hardware also comes in porcelain, ceramic, glass, plastic, and wood.

In the last five years, the biggest change on the hardware front has been the increased use of iron and weathered bronze. Several manufacturers, including Top Knob, Hafele, Amerok, and Belwith, have added rustic iron or weathered iron pulls and knobs to their lines. There are also several firms that make handmade pieces. The problem, of course, is cost. Purchasing five or six knobs for a bathroom at $25 a piece is one thing; the average kitchen requires between 30 and 60 pieces of hardware.

For a sleek, clean look, your cabinets can be fitted with invisible hardware. This type of hardware allows your cabinet fronts to be free of any embellishments. Cabinet doors can simply be opened on the hinges or may be fitted with a spring-loaded hinge that pops the door open with a gentle push on the corner.

Left: Though they both have a brushed-nickel finish, these two types of hardware have decidedly different functions. The pull on the drawer can be opened with one finger. The handle on the cabinet is curved for comfortable use and sturdy enough visually to hold up to the dark-stained cabinets.

Below, from left: Hardware can take on many forms and be made of many materials. Worn-looking embossed metal pulls are a perfect fit for the distressed finish on these vintage-style cabinets. A curved metal handle is a sleek touch on a red metal cabinet. Some homeowners embellish their cabinets with hardware that reflects personal interests, such as raising bull mastiffs (top) or—no surprise here—cooking (bottom).

Countertops and Backsplashes

Two trends seem to be influencing countertop choices these days: a preference for natural or natural-looking materials and a lack of inhibition about mixing and matching countertop surfaces. Both trends open up exciting design possibilities, and manufacturers have responded with more choices than ever. Here's a look at the latest counter offerings.

Laminate

A laminate is a $\frac{1}{16}$-inch-thick polymer layer bonded to a $\frac{3}{4}$-inch-thick plywood or particleboard. In the better varieties, the color runs all the way through the polymer sheet, helping to hide scratches and chips and eliminating the telltale brown line along the seam at the countertop edge.

Edges can be trimmed with beveled wood or metal inlays to create custom looks. A new twist is to fit laminate with edges made of solid-surfacing for corners that are rounded instead of angled. Postform laminate countertop sections are available with rolled front edges and backsplashes already attached. Laminate usually costs between $15 and $50 per linear foot installed.

Pros: Laminate is one of the least expensive countertop options. Experienced do-it-yourselfers may even be able to install the surface themselves, further reducing costs. Most appealing, perhaps, is that laminate comes in a variety of colors, textures, and patterns, making it easy to match with other kitchen elements. Laminate resists grease and soap stains and can be cleaned with soap and water.

Cons: Laminate is vulnerable to sharp knives and hot pans. Once damaged, the surface is hard to repair. In some cases, prolonged exposure to water may dissolve gluelines and cause the subsurface to warp.

Ceramic tile

A ceramic tile is a piece of fired clay. The hotter the temperature and the longer it bakes, the harder and denser it becomes, with few air pockets for moisture to penetrate. Tile dense enough for countertop is termed vitreous. It can take off-the-fire pots and pans without scorching, making it an excellent surface to place near a range, grill, or cooktop. Vitreous tile also resists moisture, so it can handle spray, splashes, and puddles around the sink.

Countertop tile may be glazed or unglazed. Glazing involves coating the tile surface with ground glass and pigments, then firing it again, making possible tile's wide range of colors and textures. Ceramic tile for countertops costs between $10 and $15 per linear foot.

Pros: The combination of incredible variety and great durability makes ceramic tile a worthy candidate for kitchen countertops. Sturdy ceramic tile comes in just about any size, shape, and color you can imagine. The potential to create patterns is ceramic tile's strong suit. You can use large field tiles and small accent tiles in contrasting colors to incorporate simple or elaborate bands, borders, and geometric shapes in your countertops.

Cons: Installing ceramic tile is a labor-intensive and potentially expensive venture. You can get a distinctive look by sprinkling a few expensive tiles into a field of economy

Below: Kitchen necessities such as a countertop and backsplash can be both functional and decorative. This metallic-finish ceramic tile backsplash mirrors the beauty of the granite countertop below it. Both materials are durable, beautiful, and timelessly appealing.

Left: The finish on soapstone countertops such as these is generally not as polished and glossy as that on granite, resulting in a more rustic look. Soapstone is slightly more porous than granite and requires more frequent sealing to guard against stains.
Below: For some homeowners, there is no substitute for tough, elegant, and virtually maintenance-free granite.

tiles; or, reserve expensive tiles for the backsplash, where they won't suffer as much day-to-day abuse.

Ceramic tile is not a great surface for cutting, particularly if the glaze is a high gloss. The tile can dull knives, and knives can scratch tile. Manufacturers usually recommend against using high-gloss glazed tiles on countertops. Unglazed tiles come in different colors as well, though usually not bright hues.

Grout lines are the Achilles' heel of ceramic tile. Although the tile itself cleans up with a damp sponge, the grouted joints between tiles collect dirt and food particles and are prone to staining, particularly light-color grouts. Grout sealants are available.

Stone

In recent years, natural stone, particularly granite, has become the most coveted kitchen countertop surface. Tough, elegant, and virtually maintenance-free, granite is the choice of those who want the very best for their kitchen and are willing to pay for it. Granite starts at a ¾-inch thickness. Costs can vary greatly, depending on the type, quality, thickness, and availability of the variety you choose. Edge treatments, such as the popular bullnose look, can add to the cost. Marble and soapstone are other natural stone choices. Granite and marble usually run between $75 and $200 a linear foot;

soapstone, which is more porous, is available for $70 per square foot.

Pros: If you can get past the sticker shock, granite rewards your investment with years of faithful service. It cleans easily; endures water, hot pots, and sharp knives unscathed; and resists most stains. The ultrasmooth surface is wonderful for rolling

out dough. Marble boasts similar qualities but, being more porous than granite, tends to stain more readily. Stone is as impervious to kitchen trends as it is to kitchen clatter—it never goes out of style. Granite, marble, and soapstone work with a variety of looks, from traditional to contemporary to country.

Cons: The greatest prohibition is the price. Even if you can find salvaged pieces at a lower price, hauling and installing the heavy, hard-to-cut slabs is costly and definitely not a do-it-yourself endeavor. Besides cost, the biggest drawback to stone countertops is lack of selection. You're limited to what nature creates on its own, and the colors and patterns tend to be subtle. Stone also is porous and requires periodic sealing.

Solid-surfacing

More resistant to scratches than laminate and less likely to stain than marble, solid-surfacing is a $\frac{1}{4}$- to $1\frac{1}{2}$-inch-thick sheet of synthetic material resembling stone that can be molded to fit any kitchen layout. Choices range from traditional stone patterns to a wide array of vivid solid colors, and special effects are possible by using inlays of contrasting colors to create borders or patterns. Solid-surfacing (Corian is the most well-known, but there are many makers, including Wilsonart and Avonite) usually costs between $100 and $150 per linear foot installed.

Pros: Solid-surfacing offers more colors and patterns than natural stone and is lighter and easier to work with.

A key feature allows your countertops and kitchen sink to be integrated, creating a seamless look that is design-friendly and aids cleanup. Solid surfacing can be routed, sandblasted, and even thermoformed into just the right shape.

Solid surfacing is nonporous and extremely durable but not indestructible. Knives and hot pots can scratch and burn the surface. However, because color runs all the way through the material, most minor damage can be repaired with an abrasive cleaner, a scouring pad, or light sanding.

Cons: In addition to the fact that it is possible to damage solid-surfacing, it carries a high price tag. Purists may think of it merely as imitation stone.

Stainless steel

An up-and-comer on the counter charts, stainless steel offers an ultra-contemporary look and appeals to serious cooks who want surfaces that will match their commercial-style appliances. Stainless steel starts at about $65 per square foot (installed) for standard sizes. Custom sizes and cutouts for sinks increase the cost.

Pros: Stainless steel is extremely durable and easy to clean, working well around stoves and sinks.

Cons: Stainless is somewhat pricey, and it does scratch. The clank of utensils on the surface can be irritating.

Concrete

Tough, reliable concrete keeps creeping further into the home, now finding favor as a countertop surface. Typically, concrete comes in large, seamless $1\frac{1}{2}$-inch-thick sections or is poured in place.

Pros: Almost as durable as more-glamorous natural stone, concrete can be colored any shade. A sealer protects the color and makes the surface easy to clean. The pigmented finish is stain-resistant.

Cons: Concrete's appearance is not terribly versatile. It's most appropriate in very contemporary kitchens because it can be industrial-looking. Also, concrete is not an easy material to replace.

Butcher block

Butcher block is made from hardwood strips—generally white oak, hard-rock maple, or beech—glued together. It comes in thicknesses $1\frac{1}{2}$ to 3 inches and can be cut into any shape. Butcher block blends well with other countertop surfaces when installed atop an island or inset in a food preparation area. Its cost starts at about $50 per linear foot.

Pros: Butcher block imparts a sense of warmth in the kitchen and makes a great cutting surface, eliminating the need for a cutting board.

Cons: Moisture is not a friend to wood, so it can't be placed near wet areas. Finishing the wood may help protect it, but some finishes are not safe for food-contact surfaces.

Below: If you want your kitchen to sparkle, consider countertops made of engineered quartz, such as this Silestone from Cosentino. Glittering flecks are a natural property of quartz.

QUARTZ

A recent innovation in engineered surfaces is the use of quartz. One of the hardest of all natural substances, quartz imparts the durability and strength found in granite. Compressed with pigments and binders in large panels, it boasts an exceptional sparkle over a range of colors not found in other stone. Its properties, and the tools and techniques required for fabrication, are closer to those of granite than solid-surfacing panels. Cosentino's Silestone and Corian's Zodiaq are examples of engineered quartz. Installed cost runs $120 to $200 per square foot.

Flooring and Finishes

Floors take a lot of punishment in the kitchen. Foot traffic is heavy, and there's exposure to water, spills, and falling objects. You need a durable surface that's easy to clean, yet stylish enough to anchor a high-visibility room. Here's how to sort out the options.

Ceramic tile

With its range of shapes and sizes, ceramic tile offers texture, durability, and potential for dynamic, colorful patterns. Recently, large formats such as 12x12, 16x16, and 24x24 inches have become more popular, which reduces the number of grout lines and the number of tiles to be installed.

Ceramic tiles are available unglazed or with a glaze that is fired onto the tile body. Fired glazes are extremely hard, but the chemical composition of the glaze and the amount of firing it receives determines whether the finished surface of the tile is delicate, tough, or somewhere in-between. Ceramic tile usually runs between $3 and $12 per square foot.

Pros: Its resistance to moisture and stains makes it an excellent choice for kitchens. Ceramic tile is also very durable, and from a design standpoint, lets you match your flooring with countertops and backsplashes.

Cons: Ceramic tile has two main drawbacks. It's hard. It also can be cold. Several companies offer electric heat tape that can be installed on the subflooring before the tile is set.

Laminate

Popular in Europe for more than two decades, plastic laminate has revolutionized home flooring in the United States in recent years.

Laminate flooring features a decorative image—most commonly wood grain—printed on one or more thin sheets of paper or other fibrous material. For durability, the decorative layer is impregnated with a plastic or resin such as melamine, subjected to high pressure, and bonded to a rigid core, resulting in a plank that's usually $5/16$ inch thick. A backing of kraft paper, resin-impregnated paper, or foil prevents warping. Laminate flooring costs between $4 and $5 a square foot.

Pros: Virtually stainproof, today's laminates are easy to clean, never fade, and never need waxing. A factory coating of aluminum oxide helps many floors resist damage from high heels, animal paws, and dropped dishes. A laminate floor simply requires damp mopping.

Cons: Because laminate flooring is relatively new, long-term performance is yet to be proved. It can sound hollow when it's walked on, though some manufacturers offer underlayments to help deaden the sound and vibration.

Laminate flooring is not totally impervious to wear. It will scratch and dent. Laminates are generally not recommended for use in high-moisture areas.

Left: The honeycomb pattern of these hexagonal terra-cotta tiles imported from Mexico is a visual treat. Tile can be glazed or unglazed. In a kitchen, unglazed tile is less slippery when wet than glazed tile—but it's also more likely to stain.
Below: Vinyl tile or linoleum doesn't have to be installed in a solid-color expanse of the same color or a checkerboard of same-size tiles. Both allow for creativity with color and pattern.

Vinyl

Vinyl (sometimes called resilient flooring) is valued for its low price, low maintenance, durability, and array of colors, patterns, and styles. Vinyl is available in two categories: rotogravure and inlaid.

Rotogravure vinyl features a knobby texture, pattern, and color printed on the finish side only. Inlaid vinyl's pattern and color run through the thickness of the material, making it more durable than rotogravure vinyl. The wear layer on rotogravure vinyl is 10 to 15 mils thick; high-quality inlaid vinyl has a 25- to 30-mils-thick wear layer.

Vinyl comes in 6- and 12-foot wide sheets and in tiles of various sizes. Vinyl tile comes with either a dry back that is laid in adhesive or a peel-and-stick backing. Vinyl flooring costs between $1 and $5 a square foot.

Pros: Vinyl has a low square-foot cost and is easy to maintain. Its resilience, or "give," means a dropped glass has a good chance of bouncing rather than breaking, and it's fairly comfortable to stand on for long periods of time.

Sheet vinyl has few or no seams, making cleaning it a breeze. If there is damage to a vinyl tile, just that tile can be replaced.

Cons: Vinyl is subject to damage from burns, high-heel shoes, or moving large appliances. The seams on vinyl tiles can trap dirt and can allow spills to filter between tiles, loosening them and damaging the subfloor. Less-expensive grades can fade and discolor quickly.

Stone

Today's stone tiles—boulders sliced into thin tiles and polished—aren't much different from those used centuries ago. Stone tiles are cut into a variety of shapes and sizes, though most come as 12-inch squares. Some feature a special surface treatment, such as a polished finish.

The most commonly used stones for tiles include granite, marble, and slate. Manufactured stone, made from hard-as-nails quartz, is the newest type of stone tile on the scene. Countertop materials Silestone and Zodiaq are both available in thinner pieces for the floor. They can be used in conjunction with counter material for a clean, uniform look. Marble or granite runs $75 to $100 per square foot; slate can be had for much less, at $3 to $12 a square foot.

Pros: Some stone tiles, such as granite, are virtually indestructible. Engineered quartz floors are extremely dense and nonporous, and are much more difficult to break than real stone. The look of a stone floor is classic and elegant.

Cons: Stone requires periodic sealing to guard against moisture absorption. Its weight prohibits it from being a do-it-yourself project. It's also very expensive.

Hardwood

Wood flooring generally consists of solid, one-piece boards of hardwood. Fear of water damage steers some away from wood flooring in the kitchen, but today's acrylic and urethane finishes offer great protection.

Red oak is the most common type of hardwood flooring, though other woods are gaining popularity. More expensive varieties include maple, ash, birch, cherry, hickory, and walnut. Imported hardwoods, such as Brazilian cherry, mahogany, and teak, also are gaining interest. Hardwood floors generally cost $6 to $14 per square foot.

Below: The raspberry-hued diamonds in this vinyl floor echo those in the ceramic tile backsplash. Vinyl flooring is valued for its economical price, easy care, resilience, and tremendous breadth of patterns and colors.

Pros: Wood flooring is warm and attractive and adds character to a kitchen. Hardwood floors last longer than vinyl and can be refinished several times, or even restained to change their appearance.

Cons: A wood floor in a kitchen is likely to have water, juice, or coffee dumped on it or have a leaky appliance spew water across it. Moisture damages wood; the shrinking and swelling (as much as $\frac{3}{8}$ inch) can pull the tongue out of the groove, compromising the integrity of the floor and causing it to buckle or warp.

Concrete

Concrete is gaining a foothold in the kitchen. Although it can be dyed in the mixing process, concrete's greatest color potential comes after it's been poured. Once smoothed, the wet concrete receives a powdered color-hardener, which is mixed in with a trowel. The color-hardener method can incorporate any color or several shades of pigment in varying amounts for a swirly, mottled effect. Basic concrete flooring costs about $4 to $10 a square foot, which includes installation.

Pros: Easy to clean, concrete can mimic natural stone at a lower cost and can be dyed any color. It's extremely durable and easy to maintain; sealing has to be done only every six to eight years.

Cons: As anyone who's ever fallen off a bicycle knows, concrete is hard. The hardness can be uncomfortable to stand on, and spells sure destruction for dropped dishes.

Linoleum

Patented in 1863 by an Englishman, linoleum—not to be confused with vinyl—is back and better than ever. To make linoleum, natural materials including linseed oil, resin, cork, limestone, and wood flour are mixed with pigments and rolled onto a jute backing and dried. As the linseed oil oxidizes, the linoleum becomes harder than vinyl. Linoleum costs about $45 or more per square yard, including installation.

Pros: Linoleum is a product made of natural components. It's far more durable than vinyl, lasting up to 40 years, and doesn't show scuffs and scratches. Linoleum cleans up easily with a damp mop.

Cons: Linoleum tiles have seam lines, which can trap dirt and moisture, and linoleum requires an occasional waxing—usually with water-based self-polishing wax—to retain its shine. It can be noisy when walked on.

Cork

The material for cork tiles—usually 12x12 inches—comes from the renewable bark of cork oak trees in Mediterranean forests. Cork tiles have a mottled grain similar to burled hardwood, and come in a variety of stains. Cork tiles cost $4 to $5 per square foot; planks cost $7 to $8. Installation costs $1 to $4 per square foot.

Pros: Cushiony cork makes a noiseless, comfortable, moisture- and temperature-resistant flooring. It can last for decades and resists damage from dropped items and even high heels. Regular maintenance is simply sweeping and mopping.

Cons: The urethane finish on cork needs to be maintained to assure easy everyday care. Every few years, the old finish needs to be sanded and new urethane reapplied.

Above: The design in a wood floor can be as simple or sophisticated as you want. This maple floor features diagonal planks around the perimeter of the room and a decorative centerpiece in a herringbone pattern. Wood flooring requires vigilance in cleaning up moisture and spills, which damage surfaces if left unattended.

Left: Stone floors are classic and elegant. Most commonly, the tiles are made from marble, slate, granite, quartz, flagstone, or limestone.

Sinks

Shopping for a kitchen sink can be complicated. There is a fountain of choices involving materials, installation methods, size, cost, color, and bowl configuration. But don't despair. Here's what you need to know about your kitchen sink.

While a standard sink is traditionally 6 to 8 inches deep, 10- to 12-inch deep sinks are gaining in popularity thanks to their ability to handle big pots and lots of dishes, and to keep water from splashing out. Whatever you choose, rest assured that there's a material out there to suit your kitchen decor, size requirements, maintenance concerns, and budget.

Materials

Cast iron: To make a cast-iron sink, molten iron is poured into a mold. An enamel coating is fired on for color, shine, and durability.

Pros: These sinks lessen noise and vibration more than many other materials, and hold water temperature longer than nearly any material.

Cons: Cast iron sinks can be extremely heavy, and the enamel coating can scratch and discolor over time. If you're interested in one of the bigger models, make sure ahead of time that your contractor is comfortable working with cast iron.

Composite: Every company seems to have its own secret recipe for composite material. Whether a sink is made of quartz, granite, or other minerals mixed with an

acrylic- or polyester-resin base, these sinks usually feature beautiful speckled color.

Pros: They're resistant to stains, dents, and scratches and are very easy to care for; just don't use an abrasive cleanser.

Cons: Composite sinks are relatively new, so their long-term track records is yet to be established; they also can be expensive.

Fireclay: As its name suggests, a fireclay sink consists of a clay base, which is fired at intense heat to produce a durable, glossy finish. Some manufacturers offer fireclay sinks with painted designs that are fired onto the surface; these add considerably to the cost.

Pros: The glazed surface resists scratches and abrasions, and it won't rust or fade.

Cons: Fireclay is somewhat porous and can stain over time.

Vitreous china: Popular for bathroom sinks and fixtures, vitreous china has made its way into the kitchen. This material is clay coated with a fired-on glaze. It is similar to fireclay in construction, durability, and cost but is less porous than fireclay.

Pros: Hard and nonporous, vitreous china boasts a glasslike shine.

Cons: The nature of the construction process makes it easier to mold larger objects, such as double-bowl kitchen sinks, out of very-similar fireclay.

Solid-surfacing: Solid-surfacing consists of a polyester or acrylic base with different ingredients used by each manufacturer. Although many manufacturers now offer ready-made models, solid-surfacing is known for its custom applications.

Pros: solid-surfacing is known for its

Left: This extra-deep, double-bowl white cast-iron sink looks like it came out of an old farmhouse; it's also a perfect fit in this more modern setting. Its generous scale makes it practical for cleaning up big pots, roasting pans, and cookie sheets; the classic style is attractive and clean looking.

DESIGNER TIP

Garbage disposals may be one of the less-glamorous aspects of your kitchen, but they sure are handy. They come in varying capacities and motor sizes, but perhaps one of the most interesting (and, certainly, quiet) developments in the last few years is the HydroMaid water-powered disposal.

It has no motor and no parts that can corrode and takes up a lot less space under the sink than a traditional disposal. It operates by turning on a water valve mounted on the counter or the sink, or even hidden inside the cabinet. As long as you have at least 40 pounds of water pressure, the water operates an internal piston that moves the five stainless blades that grind the food waste into fine particles. It can even be used with a septic system.

easy care and stonelike beauty. Available in almost every color of the rainbow—from vibrant primaries to subdued pastels, plus patterns that mimic stone—it also resists scratches and chips. Because the color runs through the entire material, minor burns or scrapes can be sanded out with relative ease.

Solid-surface sinks are usually integrated with a solid-surface countertop, which makes for a seamless and easy-to-clean set-up with no sink lip to catch crumbs.

Cons: Solid-surfacing can be nearly as expensive as granite, and though it is resistant to burns and chips, it's not completely damage-proof.

Stainless steel: Stainless steel has come a long way from its humble roots as an inexpensive builder-grade sink. There's a new generation of 16- and 18-gauge sinks that are thicker and less noisy than their less-expensive predecessors.

Stainless-steel sinks contain a percentage of chromium and nickel, which is indicated by numbers such as 18/10 (18 percent chromium and 10 percent nickel.) You also can choose a stainless-steel sink in any number of finishes, from a mirrorlike shine to a satiny luster.

Pros: The metals are corrosion resistant and add impart a rich glow to kitchen decor.

Cons: Stainless steel does scratch, and the thinner, less durable grades (such as a 21-gauge sink, for instance) can be noisy with running water and clattering dishes.

Installation

Once you've chosen your material, it's time for another decision: How should you install your sink? There are four ways:

Self-rimming: The easiest and most common method is self-rimming, so that the edge of the sink sits on top of the counter. The bowl is dropped into a hole in the countertop, the plumbing hooked up, and the edge sealed. The main drawback is that the edge of the raised sink acts as a barrier when you try to sweep crumbs into the basin, and food particles can get stuck in the seam and be difficult to clean out.

Tile-in: This method is only an option when your countertop is ceramic tile. The tiles climb right up to the edge of the sink and there is no (or very little) step-down or step-up. Apron-front sinks, which have exposed fronts, work well with this method because of their wide walls.

Undermount: Popular with solid-surfacing or stone countertops, undermount installation creates a sleek, unbroken line from counter to basin. The edge of the sink rests underneath the counter, making it look right at home in a contemporary kitchen.

Brushing scraps into the sink is a cinch. This installation method can increase labor costs because your installer must customize the countertop to suit your sink's size and shape.

Integral: Integral sinks offer an even smoother line between the countertop and sink than undermount installation. An integral sink and countertop are one piece; there's no differentiation between the two. In the past, integral sinks have been made only of solid-surfacing. However, some manufacturers now feature stainless steel as an integral option. Natural stone also is available, but with a weighty price tag.

Configuration

You no longer have to settle for the same old double-bowl sink. The options have multiplied—as has the number of basins and accessories.

Single-basin: Small kitchens might require a sink with just one bowl. Today, these are wider and deeper than ever before and can handle large pots and cutting boards with ease. Sinkmakers offer models in scads of shapes, including rectangles, ovals, circles, and combination, so you can choose a sink that adds both visual interest and convenience to your kitchen.

Double-basin: The standard two-bowl sink has received a makeover. Curved bowls add eye appeal, and configurations with one large and one small bowl allow the convenience of two bowls with the customized size most homeowners crave. Many two-basin sinks also come with one shallower side, which works well for rinsing vegetables or draining pasta. Some companies call these "one-and-a-half-basin" sinks.

Triple-basin: If you've got the space, a triple-bowl sink is a desirable indulgence. Two large basins—ideal for stacking dirty dishes—often flank one small, shallow bowl in the middle, which is good for cleaning veggies. Sink manufacturers usually offer accessories, such as colanders, cutting boards, sink grids, and drainers, that snug into the shallow basin for easy food preparation. Some of these sprawling sinks have two basins and an extra stretch of ribbed drainboard, which is perfect for stacking clean dishes to dry.

MAKING A MATCH

Like love and marriage, your sink and faucet should work as a team. When choosing mates, consider these points:
• The ideal kitchen faucet is tall enough to fill pots and can rinse all corners of your sink. One option is a faucet with a retractable head that allows you to spray water where you want it.
• To avoid splashes, make sure the faucet's height and the sink's depth are compatible. Also, check the faucet's reach: Water should flow to one side of the sink's center, but not toward the back. Extra-deep kitchen sinks and kitchen sinks with more than one basin often require special faucets to guarantee the appropriate height and reach.
• Wall-mount faucets offer the most flexibility when it comes to height. Because widespread and single-lever models can be deck-mounted, they can be positioned behind or beside sinks.
• If you need to replace a center-set faucet, consider a mini widespread version. It looks like a separate spout and handles but will fit existing center-set holes.

Faucets

Today's faucets are more stylish and dependable than ever before. Longer, taller spouts—and pullout or retractable faucets—assist you in doing a variety of kitchen tasks more quickly and easily, such as filling pasta pots or simply rinsing out the sink.

Solid-brass, die-cast innards are a sign of a high-quality faucet, but they often come with a hefty price tag—anywhere from $250 to $500 or more. Beware of faucets with plastic shells or handles. The price may be right, but their durability and resistance to scratching are likely to disappoint.

There are four basic types of faucets used in the kitchen: ceramic disk, cartridge, ball, and compression.

Single-handle, disk-type faucets operate a pair of ceramic disks that slide over each other to regulate water flow and temperature. These faucets are typically the most durable and trouble-free. The disks and mixing chamber are located in a large cylinder that is held in place with screws.

Cartridge-type faucets come in both single- and double-handle configurations. Designed for ease of repair, the flow mechanisms are housed within a cartridge that can be replaced when leaks occur.

Single-handle, ball-type faucets have a rotating ball inside the faucet that moves over water inlet holes and permits water to flow, regulates the flow of hot and cold water, and shuts off the water all together.

Compression-type faucets were common in households in the early 1900s. Double-handled, each faucet handle turns a large screw, also called a stem, inside the faucet. The stem has a washer on one end that is positioned over a hold through which the water flows. When screwed down tight, the washer fills the hole and blocks the flow of water.

As a safety precaution, some faucet models include antiscald controls that prevent the flow of water in excess of a preset temperature, usually 110 degrees. Antiscald devices can also be purchased separately and installed on existing faucets.

Left: This polished chrome gooseneck faucet is both elegant and functional: It allows ample room underneath for filling up a tall pasta pot with water or scrubbing and rinsing a large roasting pan.

WATER FILTRATION

If you have concerns about the safety, quality, taste, or odor of your drinking water, now—when you're installing a new sink and faucet—is a good time to think about adding a water-purification system to your kitchen setup. The standard water purifier has a filter installed under the sink that uses a three-stage reverse-osmosis technology to improve the quality of your drinking water. Having an undersink unit saves the time and hassle of filling up countertop models. In the first stage, tap or well water passes through a sediment filter where particles such as sand and clay are removed. The water is then forced through a carbon filter that absorbs chlorine, pesticides, and other harmful organic chemicals and pollutants. Last, the water flows into a module where pure water molecules are forced through a reverse-osmosis membrane that leaves salts, hardness, bacteria, viruses, pyrogens, and other impurities to be flushed from the system. The only drawback of this type of system is that it does waste water. For every gallon of filtered water it produces, between 2 and 4 (or more) gallons are wasted.

Cooktops, Ranges, and Ovens

The symbolic hearth at the heart of the home, the range is a major purchase. The combinations and choices are nearly limitless. You can have an all-in-one range with a cooktop and an oven; a separate cooktop and wall oven (or ovens); a standard 30-inch unit or an imposing, gleaming, 60-inch professional-style range. And that's just the beginning. Here are some things to consider when choosing cooking appliances.

Gas or electric

Many cooks prefer the greater control and visual evidence of heat levels that gas burners offer. Gas also provides the convenience of instant on and off, and it's economical. Other cooks feel electric cooking is cleaner and easier.

If you choose gas, traditional burner grates can be removed easily for cleaning. Sealed-design gas burners also prevent spills from seeping beneath them. On electric ranges, coil elements accommodate almost any cookware; glass-ceramic electric cooktops have radiant electric elements sealed beneath the surfaces and are sleek-looking and easy to clean.

Convection or thermal cooking

Convection cooking is now available in both gas and electric ranges as an option to traditional thermal (radiant) cooking. Thermal ovens use heat elements to roast, bake, and broil while convection ovens use fans to circulate heated air all around food for faster, more even cooking. Convection cooking produces crustier breads, juicier roasts, and three racks of cookies at one time.

Compare the benefits of both types of cooking and decide which best meets your family's needs. Or look for a dual-fuel range model that combines a gas cooktop with an electric oven.

Range size

Range dimensions vary slightly; measure the space you have before you shop. The standard freestanding range is 30 inches wide; restaurant-style models are available in 36-, 48-, and 60-inch widths. Remember cabinet depth: Flush cabinet installation offers an attractive, built-in look.

Range features

Easy-cleaning features: Self-cleaning ovens use a high-temperature cycle to burn food spills into a fine ash for easy wiping. Continuous cleaning ovens have textured walls to absorb and burn spatters. Cooktops are made in a variety of smooth surfaces for quick cleanup. Electronic controls have a flat surface with no knobs to wipe around.

Safety features: Range and cooktop control locks protect children. Hot-surface indicators are useful for everyone.

Convenience features: Intuitive electronic controls are logical and have easy-to-read graphics. Some ranges offer one-touch controls preset to common cooking temperatures. Delay and time-baking cycles allow you to start and stop the cooking process even when you're out.

Performance features: Look for cooktops with a mix of outputs—high-Btu power for boiling and sautéing and a simmer setting for cooking sauces and melting

Below: **If you love the old-time look of a cast-iron stove, perhaps Aga's modern-day version will suit you. Imported from England, the stove uses natural gas or propane instead of wood to create the same radiant heat for which cast-iron stoves are known. Because it takes many hours for a cast-iron cooker to heat up, this stove stays on all the time to keep its cooking elements and ovens at a constant temperature. Even though it's on all the time, it uses very little fuel for the heat it produces.**

'PRO LITE'

Have a taste for the look but can't abide the industrial-strength price of a pro-style appliance? Don't give up hope. Several residential range manufacturers, including Amana, Frigidaire, and Sears Kenmore, have taken top-end residential ranges, wrapped them in stainless steel, and added pro-look grates. The result: Style at considerably less cost (generally less than $1,500). What you lose is performance: Most 'pro lite' stoves are the standard, 30-inch wide residential size, which means you lose the option of six burners and big grills and griddles. But if residential-grade performance is all you need and professional style is important to you, they're well worth a look.

Part of the appeal of professional-style ranges is their styling. For serious cooks, they also offer a far wider selection of heat output than do standard appliances as well as options that include grills, griddles, convection ovens, and warming drawers.

chocolate. Variable-temperature broiling lets you select the ideal temperature for anything from thick steaks to delicate fish.

Durability

Ranges endure a lot of wear and tear over their 10- to 15-year lifespans, so look for heavy-duty oven racks that support roasts and large casseroles, porcelain broiler pans, and durable and dishwasher-safe grids. Expect at least a one-year warranty—five years on electronics and heating elements.

Ventilation units

The fun part may be choosing the range or oven and cooktop combination you'll purchase, but you won't enjoy cooking one bit if you can't stand to be in your kitchen because of the heat or if you're chased out of the rest of your house by residual cooking smells.

Below right: This 30-inch-wide gas cooktop with sealed burners can be installed in a countertop, island, or peninsula—over an undercounter oven, if you'd like.

Bottom: Sleek and subtle, the electric cooktop from Amana features an easy-clean glass-ceramic surface and frameless design that fits seamlessly into any countertop.

The solution to both of these concerns is a proper ventilation unit.

There are two types of ventilation systems: an updraft range hood that hangs over the cooktop and sucks up steam and odors and vents them to the outside, and a downdraft system, which is usually a vent built into the back of a cooktop. A downdraft system is not as obtrusive as an updraft system, but it's usually not as effective, because it simply filters and recirculates the air rather than getting rid of it.

The size and power of your ventilation system will be determined by the kind of cooktop you have. Most residential kitchen ventilation units move about 300 cubic feet of air or less per minute. That's fine for a standard four-burner electric or gas range or countertop unit. But commercial and professional-style ranges and burner units require larger ventilation units that can handle more heat and steam. Most of the commercial-style ranges generate between 15,000 and 16,000 Btus of heat (Btu stands for British thermal unit, a measure of heat energy). With even four burners on, that's the same 64,000 Btus that a small furnace puts out.

The ventilation requirement for commercial-style ranges is 300 cubic feet of air movement per running foot of cooking unit per minute. That means a 30-inch stove needs 750 cubic feet. A 48-inch unit requires 1,200 cubic feet of air per minute. Most of the ventilation units in that range costs more than $1,000.

Commercial-style ranges

If you cook a lot—or just want your kitchen outfitted so you can—you're probably thinking about upgrading your 30-inch residential range to something with more power, features, and finesse.

A cautionary note: True commercial ranges, the kind that gleam in the galleys of five-star restaurants, are very costly. Some have price tags in the five-figure range, meaning you could easily blow your entire kitchen remodeling budget on just one item. Add to that the package of required

accessories, including a high-capacity vent hood to exhaust the fumes and heat that the range will generate. You'd also have to come up with the side and rear clearances these uninsulated fireboxes require. And after all that, you won't even have some key convenience features, such as a self-cleaning oven, built-in broiler, or electronic ignition. In short, unless you have a mansion and a personal chef, you're probably better off with a "pro-style" range that combines much of the power, precision, and features of a commercial appliance in a user-friendly, flexible, easy-to-install package. And at around half the price of their industrial-weight counterparts, pro-style ranges leave some cash in your remodeling budget.

Above left: **A smooth cooktop range makes for easy cleaning and daily care. After it's cool, just wipe up spills with warm water and a little soap.**
Below left: **The Professional Double Wall oven from DCS fits in a standard 27-inch cabinet space and offers 3.2 cubic feet of cooking space in each oven. The four stainless steel baking racks feature easy-glide rollers.**

DESIGNER TIP

Double ovens give frequent bakers and entertainers room to cook a sumptuous holiday feast or bake a party-size batch of cheese puffs or cookies. Many new wall ovens are available with a convection option. With double ovens, you can cook food consistently at three or four rack positions and at different temperatures at the same time, and the smells from your roast won't contaminate your cake.

Above: **A ventilation hood has an important function—to expel heat, steam, and cooking odors to the exterior of the house—but it can be a decorative element, too. This massive hood imparts the warm glow of copper to the classic white kitchen and serves as a centerpiece for the room. The exterior of a ventilation hood also can be stainless steel, decoratively painted stucco, or ceramic tile.**

Pro-style ranges often feature high-capacity and simmer burners, grills and griddles, continuous grates, and convection ovens in a compact unit that fits flush into standard 24-inch-deep residential cabinetry. Most models also feature user-friendly conveniences such as self-cleaning ovens, built-in broilers, electronic controls, and pilotless ignition. They also cost between $4,000 and $9,000—so the first question you have to answer is: Do they really fit the way you want to cook?

Burner performance

Different manufacturers take different approaches to delivering professional-style performance. Many pro-style ranges have burners that generate up to 15,000 Btus, compared to the 10,000-Btu maximum of most residential ranges. These burners can boil liquids faster and sear meats more quickly. Thanks to their larger

flame area, they also tend to heat more evenly. To distribute the heat, some manufacturers use a star-shape burner, others a dual-ring configuration.

On the other end of the heat scale, most residential ranges produce a minimum of 1,000 Btus. Some commercial-grade simmer burners can be turned down to produce half that much heat or even less for delicate culinary jobs such as melting chocolate. Dual-ring burners accomplish this feat by shutting off the outer burner ring; star-shape burners simply reduce the flame size or cycle on and off.

You'll also find another classification for burners: sealed and open. Sealed burners keep spills confined to the stovetop for easy cleanup. Open burners have drip trays that slide out for cleaning. Proponents of open burners claim they heat faster and adjust more precisely because of greater air supply for the burner flame. Others appreciate the convenience of sealed burners.

Pro-style ranges offer a variety of cooktop configurations as well. On most 36-inch-wide ranges, there's room for six burners, if you like. If four are plenty, you can often equip the cooktop's middle section with a griddle or grill.

Next stop: ovens

Precise heat control on these models is handled by thermostats that keep oven settings to within 10 degrees of the setting for near-perfect baking. Because electric ovens maintain a somewhat steadier temperature than gas units, some stoves are dual-fuel, offering the speed and precision of gas burners with the more even heat of an electric oven. These units typically cost about 20 percent more than their all-gas counterparts. Some upscale 30-inch residential ranges also offer this option.

Virtually all pro-style ranges feature convection ovens. There are differences here, too. All models feature a fan mounted in the rear panel, but American-style convection ovens circulate heat from the lower element, while European-style or "true convection" systems employ a third element that surrounds the fan, so the air is heated just prior to recirculation.

The advantage, say proponents of the European system, is more even heat and less mixing of flavors when cooking more than one type of food at a time.

Above: If preparing healthy meals fast is a priority, consider a convection steam oven, such as this one from Miele. The steam cooking doesn't require oils or sauces, and it seals in vitamins and minerals that are necessary for good health. The oven is designed with multiple chambers so you can cook different foods at different temperatures— most of which take less than 20 minutes to cook in a convection oven.
Left: A cooktop in an island allows for a built-in griddle. All cooktops must be outfitted with a system for venting out steam, grease, and heat; this one has a downdraft system.

Right: **Dishwashers can be fitted with wood panels that mask their location in the cabinetry—or, as in the case of this model—they can be visually integrated into the base cabinets in a decorative way. This one was fitted with a stainless-steel panel framed by wood that echoes the stainless-steel drawers also surrounded by a wood frame.**

Dishwashers

Dirty dishes can ruin a great meal, but how do you know that a dishwasher won't let you down? With dishwasher prices ranging from $200 to more than $1,500, it's vital to know which features you really need. Consider these features and amenities as you shop for a dishwasher for your kitchen.

Size and type

If you're shopping for a new installation, measure the space and take the dimensions with you to the dealer. You can choose between built-in and portable, and full-size or compact models.

Noise levels

If family activities and conversations take place in or near the kitchen, a noisy dishwasher is irritating. The best way to reduce sound is to add or improve insulation around the washing tub, door, toe panel, and access panels. Some models offer extra-quiet motors and vibration-absorbing materials, but you will pay more for those features.

Saving energy

If you always choose the highest wash cycle, you'll use more hot water and energy. Consider other cycles that use less energy and water—as little as 4 gallons—when dishes are less soiled. A delay-start control lets you wash during less-costly off-peak hours. Read the Energy Guide labels for operating costs.

TOP DRAWER: KEEP IT CLEAN

Here's a dishwasher that can handle big and small loads economically. The Fisher & Paykel DishDrawer's two-compartment design lets each drawer operate independently or in tandem as a single unit. That means you can run a small load if you need to, and you'll use as little as 2.4 gallons of water. Wash pots and pans in one drawer, delicate crystal using a different cycle in the other. Or load and unload drawers in sequence so you always have clean dishes.

User-friendly features

Angled control panels, large digital displays, wide push buttons, and soft-touch electronic controls are among the design elements you'll want to investigate. Consider elevating your dishwasher 12 to 18 inches, if possible, to minimize bending as you load and unload it. Inside, several models use sensors to measure the soil content of the water and adjust wash cycles to suit. Be sure that detergent and rinse additive dispensers are large enough and conveniently located.

Performance appraisal

Look again at the number and type of wash cycles to take care of everything from your grandma's crystal to greasy casseroles as well as the sprayer mechanism's design. High-performance dishwashers have two or three spray arms that soak dishes with water from several levels and angles. In the spray arms, smaller holes tend to emit a more forceful spray. A central wash tower may improve washing performance, but you'll lose some rack space.

A twin-pump system drains dirty water faster than a standard single pump. Wash-water filters and internal food disposers are common on many models. Less common is a booster that heats rinse water to help sanitize dishes without setting your home's water heater higher.

Racks

Dish and glass racks are basically metal wires coated with nylon or vinyl. The tops of tines wear first; check the coverage in those areas. Adjustable-height racks add flexibility when you need to load large items or serving pieces. If you like to entertain, you'll appreciate models that hold 12 place settings (most hold 10). Special baskets, hooks, and trays are designed for knives, cooking utensils, and lightweight plastic items that might fly around during washing.

Longevity

Dishwasher tubs are made from plastic, porcelain-enameled metal, or stainless steel. Plastic resists chipping and rusting better than enameled metal, but it can discolor.

Stainless-steel washtub interiors are durable and easy to rinse and clean, and the finish resists nicks, chips, stains, and odor buildup. Stainless stands up to abuse, so it looks new for a long time, and its natural sheeting action saves drying time.

Exteriors

High-end dishwasher models are available in the restaurant-style look. If you want your dishwasher to disappear, look for a built-in model with the option of adding trim panels to match your cabinets. Some manufacturers have moved controls from the front to the top of the door to further disguise the appliance.

Left: Some homeowners love the polished gleam of stainless steel and make no attempt to hide the dishwasher's location. **Below:** Others prefer to disguise it in the cabinetry. This white-wood paneled model from Asko is so well-disguised it's difficult to find it at first glance. Molding and hardware that match the cabinets make for a seamless look.

Refrigerators and Freezers

Day in and day out, the refrigerator is the kitchen's workhorse, and it's used by every member of the family. Today's cold storage is packed with cool features, but before you spend $400 to $5,000, it's wise to ponder your family's refrigerator priorities.

Configurations

The most popular configuration for a refrigerator-freezer unit is the two-door, top-freezer design. Bottom-freezer units put fresh food at eye level and frozen items below. Side-by-side models have narrow doors that open at the center. They generally offer more storage capacity and easier access for children or people in wheelchairs but don't accommodate items very well.

Space requirements

Refrigerators vary in size and the clearance space they require. Measure the height, width, and depth of the space for your refrigerator and take these dimensions with you when you shop. Shallow models that extend from the wall about as far as standard cabinet fronts look better than models that bump out beyond countertops, blocking traffic flow or a doorway.

Capacity

Refrigerator sizes range between 9 and 30 cubic feet. A family of two generally needs 8 to 10 cubic feet of fresh food space.

Add an extra cubic foot for each additional family member. Refrigerators can operate for 15 years or more, so remember to plan for changes in family size.

A family of two needs about 4 cubic feet of freezer space. Add 2 more cubic feet for each additional person. Increase the freezer

Right: Although most refrigerators are made with the freezer on top, consumers increasingly are buying those with the freezer on the bottom. This common-sense configuration puts fresh food at eye level and frozen foods below, which means no bending and bowing your back to look into the refrigerator.

Below right: Wine refrigerators, outfitted with racks that store wine in the recommended horizontal position (so the corks don't dry out and let air in, which can ruin the wine), keep wines at the perfect serving temperature.

TOP DRAWERS: KEEP IT COLD

Do you ever think one refrigerator isn't enough? Wouldn't it be convenient to add a smaller model within your kitchen island to store foods you prepare there, or in an exercise room or the family room to keep drinks and snacks handy?

Several refrigerator manufacturers now make refrigerator drawers that fit neatly into the cabinetry. You can stack them for a traditional refrigerator configuration, or use them alone. Drawers are fully built in and hinges are hidden; add hardware to match surrounding cabinets.

space if you buy a lot of frozen products or shop infrequently. Top- and bottom-mount freezers offer the most storage flexibility. Side-by-side models may offer more storage space, but sometimes it's tricky to wedge in a pizza, party tray, or other large items.

Interior features

Adjustable-height glass shelves make room for foods of any size and shape and better reveal what you're hungry for. Spill-proof shelves reduce cleanup time; look for shelves that lift all the way out for washing in the sink. Large, adjustable door bins are essential for easy access to gallon-size milk, juice, and soft drinks. Spacious crispers with clear fronts and adjustable humidity controls help you keep track of the fruits and vegetables you buy, and foods will stay fresh longer. In the freezer, slide- and tilt-out baskets are handy.

Icemakers

Some refrigerator/freezer models already have icemakers built into the freezer at the factory. In other models, icemaker kits can be installed quickly.

Once you've used a through-the-door ice and water dispenser, it's hard to imagine life without one. Most useful for children or people who frequently get cold drinks, these devices also save energy—no warm air enters

the interior of the unit. High-end refrigerators often include built-in water filters that help the dispensed ice and water look and taste better.

Refrigerator style

There are several options for the look of your refrigerator. Attention-getting stainless steel has made tremendous inroads in the last few years, as have restaurant-style glass doors and wood front-trim panels that blend the mass of the refrigerator into the surrounding cabinets. White and almond remain the most popular colors, but black is striking and may be ideal if you want to match other black appliances.

Noise and energy issues

When you're in the store, ask that a few models be turned on so you can hear how they sound. The noise will be quieter in your kitchen than on a concrete sales floor. Check each model's yellow Energy Guide label to determine the average energy use per year. Make sure the models you compare are the same capacity.

Left: There is a refrigerator to suit every space. Even a tiny kitchen can boast loads of cold storage with this tall and narrow unit from Northland. It has nearly 5 cubic feet of freezer space and more than 10 cubic feet of refrigerator space—and only takes up 4 square feet of floor area. The "quilted" stainless steel front adds an eye-catching accent to the room.

Below: Refrigerators that sit flush with the cabinets, such as this large-capacity stainless-steel side-by-side, don't jut out into the room and interfere with traffic flow.

Lighting

Lighting in your kitchen needs to be both functional—so you can see what you're doing—and mood-setting. After all, this is the room that serves as a gathering place and party center. A lighting plan that addresses general lighting, ambient lighting, task lighting, and accent lighting will serve you and your cooking and dining space best.

Here are some tips for creating a well-lit, cheerful spot to prepare food, eat meals, and chat with family and friends.

Overhead lighting pours light over the entire room. Well-placed lighting from ceiling-mounted fixtures, track lights, or recessed cans provides good overall illumination. Scatter fixtures throughout the room so they pool light where you need it most: over the sink, near the oven, and on the countertops. In kitchens larger than 120 square feet, two or more ceiling-mounted fixtures may be needed.

Right: Lighting fixtures aren't purely functional; many of them make a style statement in and of themselves. These glowing, cobalt-blue pendant lights provide illumination over the island—and spark up the kitchen with a splash of vivid color.

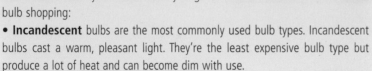

BULB BAZAAR

Most lighting designs are created for a particular type of light bulb. Most light bulb designs are made in a variety of shapes and sizes. Here's what you'll find when you go bulb shopping:

• **Incandescent** bulbs are the most commonly used bulb types. Incandescent bulbs cast a warm, pleasant light. They're the least expensive bulb type but produce a lot of heat and can become dim with use.

• **Tungsten-halogen** bulbs are a low-voltage, pricier type of incandescent bulb that produce an intense beam of light ideal for accent lighting. Halogen bulbs don't dim with age, can last four times as long as incandescent bulbs, and use less electricity, too. Their light beams can produce an intense amount of heat, so plan to use them away from fabrics, paper, and flammable materials. Also, halogen bulbs have to be handled carefully. Direct contact with skin will contaminate them, damage the glass, and cause them to burn out rapidly.

• **Xenon** bulbs have come on the market in recent years, offering the brightness of halogen bulbs without the intense heat and delicate handling requirements. Like halogens, Xenon bulbs are low voltage and energy efficient but pricey.

• **Fluorescent** bulbs can be a budget-savvy choice. While fluorescents cost more than incandescents, they use just a third of the electricity and ultimately cost less over time. They last longer in fixtures that aren't turned off and on frequently. For the most pleasing light quality, look for color-corrected or warm white bulbs.

Natural light from windows and skylights makes the most of Mother Nature's sunshine by bringing it inside. Depending on the weather, these panes can bring in bright beams or soft, filtered light. Install curtains or blinds to control the amount of light that comes in. Windows reveal views of the backyard or other outdoor scenes, which are pleasant sights while chopping veggies or rolling out dough.

Task lights, such as small pendants or individual recessed cans over the island or sink, throw a spotlight on the work at hand. Pendants can be as beautiful as they are practical, and many people choose lights that reflect their personalities and the character of the kitchen. Recessed cans with eyeball trims can direct light to specific areas.

Undercabinet lights function as task lights for the countertop. Hidden beneath upper cabinets, these recessed fixtures are usually controlled by a switch on the backsplash and make any work on the counter much easier to see. Low-voltage halogen "hockey puck" lights can be hidden in the undercabinet recess; track lights also work and can be directed toward the task at hand. An inexpensive option for lighting the countertop utilizes slimline fluorescent fixtures; be sure to install warm-white bulbs for a more natural look.

In-cabinet lights illuminate and make gleam whatever you have stored in glass-door cabinets—usually pretty dishes and glassware. In-cabinet lighting keeps glass-door cabinets from looking like black holes and makes the whole kitchen glow.

Side lighting is the most commonly ignored type of lighting. Wall sconces, which diffuse light outward (not up or down), eliminate the hard shadows that ceiling-mounted fixtures can create. One or two well-placed sconces, for example, by the telephone or near the microwave oven, produce face- and food-flattering light.

Ambient lighting, produced by fixtures mounted in the soffit or above upper cabinets, imparts a rich glow to the room. This type of light can emphasize a striking ceiling treatment, such as textured paper or tiles, or merely supplement the main overhead lighting.

Dimmer switches are a must for kitchen fixtures. They allow you to adjust light levels throughout the day. At dinner, keep them bright to ward off the darkness outside. At night, when the kitchen is not in use, lower the lights for ambience or

maintain the soft glow to guide thirsty children in the quest for a glass of water.

New lighting designs are always being introduced, so visit lighting supply stores and showrooms to get a sense of the most recent possibilities. You'll be dazzled, if likely a bit overwhelmed, by the number of choices. Take your kitchen plans with you for expert advice about fixtures that could work and where they should be placed.

Above: **A strip of tiny undercabinet lights makes countertop tasks easy to see and cookbooks easy to read; it also creates a decorative accent—a "necklace" under the cabinetry.**
Left: **This kitchen is awash in light from several sources. There's ample natural light streaming in the bank of windows, overhead light from recessed cans in the ceiling, a food- and face-flattering chandelier over the dining area, and glowing in-cabinet lighting to display personal treasures.**

Above: **Even if you don't have a bayside view, take advantage of the beautiful views you do have and add windows to your kitchen wherever possible. This is an example of a specialty picture window. The muntins, or grilles, give the window a more traditional look than a large expanse of glass would.**

Windows

Fresh air, beautiful views, and natural light are key in any room of the house, but in the kitchen, they take on special importance.

The kitchen, after all, is the place you come in the morning to wake up with a cup of coffee. Bountiful sunlight streaming into the space is sure to give your day a cheery start. At the opposite end of the clock, consider watching the sun go down over dinner. And when somebody burns a piece of toast, an ample number of working windows helps eliminate the smoke and smell.

An ideal time to enlarge, add, or reconfigure windows is during a kitchen remodeling. Add a bay window with a garden view in a bump-out designed for eating.Install skylights overhead. Enlarge the over-the-sink window so you can enjoy even more of the outdoors as you scrub the pots and pans.

Window shopping

Like many products for our homes, windows just aren't what they used to be—and in this case, that's a good thing. Refined materials and improved details in today's versions put a lot more control at your fingertips. Not only can you get a wider variety of standard shapes, sizes, and designs, but the product is more likely to be engineered for performance levels that older windows just can't match.

For starters, here's a look at the five most common window categories:

Double-hung and single-hung: This traditional design is still the most common for new construction and remodeling. Double-hung windows feature a pair of moveable sashes that slide vertically within the window frame; single-hung models also feature an upper and lower sash, but only the lower sash is operative. (Because production volume typically is higher for double-hungs, single-hung windows usually offer little or no cost advantage.)

Older versions of either type kept the windows open by means of cords, pulleys, and counterweights, but nowadays tensioned spring systems perform that function. Appropriate for all but the most cutting-edge contemporary home designs, double-hung and single-hung windows can be found on traditional Cape Cods and colonials, multistory Victorians, early 20th-century bungalows, and other "period" architectural styles. Muntin, or grille, designs provide strong stylistic cues, but the basic design remains versatile.

Casement: Casement windows pivot on hinges, somewhat as doors do, but they usually swing outward and are controlled by a hand-crank mechanism affixed to the windowsill. Casement shapes tend toward the tall and narrow, so wide wall openings usually feature multiples, sometimes with a fixed picture window in the center. Ventilation is generous relative to the overall window area because the entire sash swings open, but exposure of the outward-swinging frame can be a problem if rain arrives suddenly.

Ranch-style, Prairie-style, and other 20th-century home designs often feature this type of window. Grilles help create a traditional look, while an unbroken expanse of glass provides a contemporary flavor.

Awning: This is another type of hinged window, but one that pivots at the top. With their horizontal rather than vertical orientation, awnings don't open as fully as casements, but they offer the advantage of shedding water harmlessly if left open during a rainfall.

Though they can be used alone, awning windows often are installed above or below large picture windows to provide ventilation at the top or bottom of a wall.

Like casements, awning windows take on a more traditional flavor when fitted with muntins but look contemporary when left unadorned.

Gliding: The principle of a gliding window, where one or two sashes slide horizontally in the tracks of a window frame, has a long history that includes Japanese shoji and other long-established uses. Still, the modern-day gliding window doesn't lend itself to such traditional designs as Cape Cod or Victorian-style homes. As with awning windows, gliders have a strong horizontal orientation, so they often work best with home designs such as ranches or Prairie-style buildings that have strong horizontal lines.

Picture: They don't get any simpler than this. Picture windows are stationary (inoperative) windows used for light and views only. They don't have to be large but often are. When maximum views are the objective, a picture window offers the least obstruction. Ventilation requirements are often handled by installing operative windows above, below, or alongside a picture window.

As with other window types, picture windows impart a decidedly modern feel when they're large and uninterrupted by muntin grilles. Smaller picture windows with grilles and appropriate trim can imitate most traditional looks.

Just about anything outside these five basic categories qualifies as a specialty window. This term refers mostly to unusual shapes, such as triangular, round, half-round, and other nonstandard configurations. Most are fixed-sash (inoperative) and are included to create architectural interest.

Other specialty windows include bow and bay windows, preassembled groupings that change the profile of an exterior wall.

Though substantially more costly than standard windows, these variations provide more light and ventilation in a given amount of wall area; create a more spacious feel and room for shelves, window seats, and other features; and add a lot of charm.

Left: A south-facing greenhouse window is a perfect place to grow beautiful blooms or cultivate an indoor herb garden. Specialty windows that change the profile of an exterior wall—such as this one or a bow or bay window—are expensive but make the kitchen feel decidedly more spacious.

Window materials

With a few exceptions for southern geographic regions and economy-grade product lines, virtually any good-quality window gets fitted with insulated glass. This means the glazing is a sandwich of two panes of glass separated by "warm channel" spacers. The spacers act as thermal breaks to keep the exchange of inside and outside temperatures to a minimum, and the voids between the panes are sometimes filled with argon gas, which offers better insulating properties than ordinary air. Unless you're ordering custom windows to get a certain size or look, the standard units you buy will likely be dual-glazed, argon-filled, and perhaps have a low-E coating (for low emissivity, which inhibits the transfer of radiant solar heat) on the glass.

Above: Take a traditional over-the-sink window to new heights. This "wall of windows" makes the cook and cleanup crew feel as if they're accomplishing their kitchen tasks in the great outdoors.

Of course, the frame components that secure the glazing give the window its structure and operation. Wood has been, by far, the traditional and most common material for the jambs, sash frames, sill, and trim, but maintenance requirements and the inevitable problems with water and sun damage have brought changes to that status. Protecting wood with a weatherproof covering called cladding eliminates the need for painting and also protects the window from the elements.

There are two types of cladding: vinyl or aluminum. Vinyl offers the advantages of excellent impact resistance and integral color, so scratches on the surface won't expose the layer underneath. You have to accept a limited number of color choices from most manufacturers, though—often white, a dark taupe (neutral brown), and a lighter neutral (beige) color.

Aluminum cladding requires more care in handling to avoid scratches or dents, but the factory-applied paint finishes are extremely durable and typically come in at least a dozen colors.

Either way, you lose the flexibility of changing the color later and keeping the same low-maintenance feature. The interior surfaces of these windows are finish-grade wood that can be stained or painted. Clad-wood windows account for about 90 percent of the wood-frame window market, although wood windows with primed or raw exteriors are available from several makers.

Some manufacturers do without wood entirely, opting for frame components made of aluminum or solid vinyl. Though less expensive, these have their drawbacks, too. Aluminum is a poor insulator and vinyl lacks the rigidity of either wood or aluminum, so the frames flex more and move in response to temperature swings.

Recently, wood composites (a mix of shredded wood fiber and plastic resins) have become more common for the structural core of window frames and components. These compounds are extruded into hollow tube shapes, then covered with vinyl or aluminum exterior cladding and a paint primer or vinyl cladding on the interior. This approach capitalizes on the strength and insulating properties of wood but doesn't require the expensive, high-grade materials used in solid-wood frames, providing a cost savings; however, you can't use a transparent stain on interior surfaces.

Depending on what features and materials you choose, a 30×48-inch window, for example, costs from about $80 to $185. With windows, as in the case of many things, you often get what you pay for. Energy efficiency and a no-maintenance exterior will offset the up-front cost over time. Installation and labor costs could be higher for an economy-grade window if you factor in charges for painting. And if your economy-grade windows are leaking and rotten in just a few years and have to be replaced, they were no bargain at all.

Comparative Costs

Cabinets (Per linear foot)	$50 to $200 for fixed-size stock (ready-made), limited finish and door style selection $150 to $400 for semicustom (fixed sizes with fill-in panels to fit space available), broad choice of finishes and styles $250 to $1,000 for custom (any size, shape, style, finish you want)
Countertops (Per linear foot) (Per square foot)	$15 to $50 for laminate, ceramic tile $80 to $150 for solid-surfacing $50+ for butcher block $75 to $200 for marble, granite $10 to $20 for stainless steel $60 to $130 for concrete
Flooring (Per square foot)	$1 to $5 for vinyl tile or vinyl sheet flooring $3 to $12 for ceramic tile, slate $4 to $5 for laminate $5 to $8 for cork $6 to $14 for hardwood $75 to $100 for marble and granite
Sink	$100 to $200 for enameled steel $150 to $400 for acrylic $200 to $1,200 for cast iron or solid-surfacing $65 to $2,000 for stainless steel $750 to $1,200 for apron-front ("farmhouse") style
Faucet	$50 to $150 for basic chrome with plastic cartridge $150 to $350 for solid brass, ceramic-disk valves, chrome/color finish, pullout spout $200 to $350 for brass, nickel, copper, pewter, brushed, matte finishes, pullout spout $500 to $600 for contemporary wall-mount design
Garbage Disposal	$75 to $100 for a basic, batch-feed model $300 to $350 for a top-of-the-line, high-power, quiet-running, continuous-feed model
Trash Compactor	$500 to $900
Range (cooktop and oven are one unit)	$300 to $500 for basic 30-inch model, electric or gas $400 to $600+ for self cleaning, smooth top glass or sealed burners $1,000 to $2,000 for dual fuel $4,000 to $9,000 for professional style
Oven	$400 to $1,000 for basic, single model slide-in or built-in $1,000 to $1,500 for double, self-cleaning $2,000+ for single, microwave/convection combination
Cooktop	$250 to $300 for basic four-burner model, electric or gas $450 to $1,200 for glass, ceramic, radiant, halogen $2,500 to $3,500 for high-powered professional grade
Ventilation Hood	$75 to $150 for basic hood fan, light $500 to $1,000 for premium updraft, downdraft $500 to $1,000 for slide-out $1,000 to $5,000 for high-capacity, suitable for professional-caliber range
Microwave Oven	$80 to $100 for basic countertop model $200 to $400 for high-powered, programmable with turntable $600 to $1,000 for built-in
Dishwasher	$300 to $400 for basic model, plastic or enameled-steel interior $600 to $800 for midrange with built-in disposer, pot-scrubber cycle, programmable feature $1,000 to $2,000 for stainless-steel interior, ultraquiet feature
Refrigerator-Freezer	$500 to $600 for basic model, freezer on top $600 to $1,200 for side-by-side $1,000 to $1,500 for 22-cubic-foot model, top-mount with slide-out shelves $2,400 to $4,000 for built-in or commercial style

Decorating Your Kitchen

The contractor's gone and the dust is cleaned up. It's time to put the finishing touches on your kitchen.

Opposite: Decorative details such as an art-glass inset and a patterned tile floor that mimics the look of a rug were built into this country-style kitchen. The lovely lavender color and lighthearted accessories such as the rug and painted barstools give it a touch of whimsy.

More and more, the kitchen opens up to or flows into other living space, such as a family room or living room. These days, the kitchen is a room that isn't just used but lived in. Consequently, kitchens are being decked out, decorated, and personalized very much as the rest of the house has always been.

When you're remodeling your kitchen, you can build in decorative and architectural details such as pillars and columns, a tile pattern on the floor, or a beautiful backsplash that adds to its beauty. This chapter is about what comes after that—about the ephemeral and changeable elements that make your kitchen the heart of your home. Your personal preferences in color, pattern, and furnishings make your kitchen a welcoming place that's lovely to look at, and truly a place you want to be three times a day—and much more often than that.

Color Conscious

Colors come and go in popularity and are highly subject to personal preference. There are some color schemes, however, that have stood the test of time. The most classic is the all-white kitchen.

White, often accented with one color such as blue, is a popular choice for the kitchen because it's clean-looking and helps visually downplay the dirty dishes, pots-and-pans clutter that a kitchen is naturally prone to. Kitchens are also expensive, and white never goes out of style. The only downside of an all-white kitchen is that is can look sterile and cold, but that's easily fixed with the addition of warm-toned elements, such as a honey-colored wood floor, or soft accents such as curtains at the windows or an upholstered banquette seat.

Even an all-white kitchen has color in it: An oak floor infuses it with yellow, a granite countertop can be gray, pink, green, or black. Keep in mind, too, that there are

hundreds of whites; white can be warm or cool—it can even be hot.

True colors—as opposed to white, which is a neutral—are generally considered warm or cool. Warm colors, such as tones of red, yellow, and orange, are energizing. Cool colors, such as blue, green, and violet, are calming. Color does indeed affect mood. Studies have shown that exposure to red, for instance, quickens the pulse and breathing rate and increases the appetite. Any color can be used with great success in the kitchen if you follow a few color guidelines.

Generally, it is wise to pick one color as an overall or base color and then one, or maybe two at the most, as accent colors. Complementary colors—those that sit opposite one another on the color wheel—intensify each other and impart the space with energy. Analogous colors—those that sit next to one another on the color wheel—are visually softer together, and will make the space seem more serene. Neutrals such as taupe, tan, black, white, cream, and shades of gray can be a color scheme in and of themselves, or can be paired with nearly any color as an accent.

When thinking about what kind of a color scheme you'd like for your kitchen, think not only about your favorite colors, but also those that run through a favorite quilt, in the blue-and-white willowware dishes you inherited from your grandmother, or in a beloved painting. Perhaps your color inspiration will come from the walls of a

villa you visited in Tuscany, an adobe you admired in Mexico, or a cottage garden you strolled through in England. Choose a color scheme based on something you love and you'll never tire of it.

Color trends

All visual arts are subject to the vagaries of fashion. One trend that doesn't seem to be going away any time soon is the use of natural materials and elements such as wood, stone, and metal in the kitchen. Colors that complement these materials also are coming to the forefront of the design world—namely, the spice tones of paprika, mustard, cinnamon, oregano, and sage—and what more appropriate palette for the kitchen?

Warm spice tones blended with a touch of cool, clear sea tones conjure up exotic images of the Far East, India, Africa, and the Aegean Sea. These colors combine to create a wonderful design contradiction—a space that's as lush and elegant as it is comfortable and inviting.

Think of traditional textiles dyed by natural, centuries-old methods and showcased alongside the bright, colorful tiles of a Turkish patio and you have today's spice palette.

So why not consider the rich red found on textiles in a Marrakesh marketplace or the pale gold of a lush Indian sari as the basis for your next kitchen color foray? Even softer shades of basil, oregano, and sage play nicely off cinnamon and cumin tones to create unique recipes for a plush space that will deliver the ultimate in comfort.

If you do grow weary of it in a few years, paint is certainly an easy thing to change and is a great way to get a fresh look.

Left: Although there are three very saturated colors used in this kitchen, it still looks clean and airy, thanks to a sparing use of pattern. The main color, green, sets a serene tone, despite the vivid bursts of yellow and apricot that serve to make the space bright and fun.

PLEASING PATTERNS

Because the kitchen is a busy place with lots going on visually, it's generally a good idea to use pattern fairly sparingly, and to keep what is used clean and simple. Geometrics such as checks (think of the classic checkerboard floor), ginghams, stripes, and plaids are always good choices, as are airy florals and classics such as Provençal-style prints and toiles.

Natural materials such as wood and stone (and fabricated materials that mimic natural materials such as laminate and some solid-surfacing) have patterns of their own that are generally subtle and will blend with nearly any other pattern.

Furnishings

Below: Think out of the box: This kitchen table is fitted with a collection of mismatched dining chairs found at antiques shops and tag sales. The result is artful and visually interesting.

After the cabinetry, of course, the primary furnishings in a kitchen are the pieces that comprise the dining arrangement. A peninsula or island for casual meals begs for casual seating: Barstools, either round or square, with backs or not, and with seat cushions or not. If you have the space and inclination, a kitchen table is more comfortable for eating because you don't have to climb up into the chair and you can face your dining companions.

Study the style you've chosen for your kitchen and use it to guide you in picking an appropriate dining set. Perhaps it's a 1950s-style laminate table with easy-wipe vinyl-padded chairs, or maybe it's a marble-topped table with Italian-country-style ladderback chairs fitted with rushed seats.

Mix a distressed pine table with painted chairs—or use an eclectic mix of one-of-a-kind chairs you've discovered at antique shops and tag sales.

There is no rule that says you must march out the minute you pay the contractor and buy a brand-new dinette set with matching table and chairs. If that's what pleases you, by all means do it. But dining furniture creates an intimate space for eating and conversing with family and friends; it should speak volumes about who you are. What you already have may be ideal.

Box seats

Coming in all shapes and styles, box seats strike our fancy for the same reasons we choose a booth instead of a table at restaurant: privacy, intimacy, camaraderie, even romance. If you've ever dined at a table

Above: **The layout of this home—the kitchen opens to the dining room and the dining room to the living room—requires that each room maintain a distinct character that reflects its use but also that the furnishing style blends well so the rooms flow into one another.**

BANQUETTE BASICS

Besides the standard restaurant booth setup, banquette options include U-shapes, L-shapes, semicircles, and hybrids combining bench seats and chairs. Although box seats work especially well in recessed areas, you can build one flush against the wall, too. A booth for four with fixed seating can fit into a 42x60-inch space. Here are other considerations:

• Standard table height and width is 30 inches. Allow 12 inches from the top of the benches to the table surface; benches should be 18 inches high. Let the table overlap the benches by 3 or 4 inches on each side. For more legroom, set the benches back a few inches and add a "heel kick" on the floor below the table overlap.

• Allow a minimum of 21 inches of table and seating length per person. Also allow for 18 inches of seating depth, not counting the back support.

• Allow 54 inches for each leg of the U and 78 inches for the rear bench. U-shapes need more generous dimensions to avoid knee-squeezing corners.

• Leave plenty of vertical clearance for a hanging light fixture. Bumped heads can result if a fixture is placed too low over a booth.

ISLAND STYLE

Some islands serve as seating for casual meals, some purely as work surfaces and storage. Some are stationary; others can be brought in rather than built-in. Some are technically peninsulas, or extensions of the countertop. Nearly anything with a virtually indestructible foodsafe surface that's at a comfortable height for food prep and eating can serve as an island: an antique stove fitted with a countertop, a rustic pine farm table, a mahogany library table, or a marble-topped baker's table.

in the middle of a crowded restaurant, you know the uneasy feeling of being "on stage." In that same setting, a booth lets you forget your surroundings and focus on your dining companions.

Although privacy isn't a concern in your own kitchen, a charming banquette does inspire the same kind of physical closeness and sense of fun and fellowship you experience when dining out. Booth seating begs an informal atmosphere, inviting us to spread out (or squeeze together), put our elbows on the table, and just enjoy the meal.

If carefully placed and designed, a banquette does even more, making the most of precious kitchen floor space, providing convenient storage above and below the seats and saving time and energy in serving meals. Why run yourself ragged going back and forth between the kitchen and the dining room when a banquette puts the table just a few steps from the stove?

In a larger kitchen, box seats can be a miniature dining room, a haven separate from the work area. In a smaller space, even a lowly alcove, window, or wasted corner can be the perfect spot to squeeze in seating for four. Because you don't have to pull out any chairs, you don't need as much clearance for a banquette as you do with a traditional table. Less chair sliding gives your floor a

break too. From a style standpoint, box seats add warmth and personality to your kitchen with the colors and materials you choose for cushions, eating surface, surrounding walls, and window treatments.

As an integral part of the room's design, a banquette is a constant reminder that your kitchen isn't just for cooking—it's also for eating.

Beyond the kitchen table

If you want to create the furnished, unfitted look in your kitchen that is so popular today, consider limiting the number of built-in base and wall cabinets and substitute one-of-a-kind pieces such as an old armoire or buffet for storing dishes,

Right: Sometimes a piece of furniture can be highly functional and very visual at the same time, as is the case with this painted buffet with a flower-motif hardware.

Left: When decorating your kitchen, consider not only what you'll be using and looking at when you're in the kitchen—but also the view you have from the kitchen. With its use of natural materials and warm, neutral colors, the interior of this kitchen blends beautifully with the picture-frame perspective of the dining room.

cookware, and foodstuffs. They can be retrofitted with either stationary or pullout shelving to make them more efficient and functional for the modern kitchen. Mix painted pieces with wood, metal, or laminate. Consider a freestanding bookshelf for your cookbook collection, and include a comfortable chair for reading, planning menus, or taking a rest.

A caveat: The kitchen, with its inevitable grease, steam, drips, and spills is not the ideal place to use upholstered furniture with abandon. If you want upholstery in the kitchen use it sparingly, be sure fabrics have been treated to resist stains, and take care that material is easy to clean. Machine-washable slipcovers for dining chairs are one option to consider.

DESIGNER TIP

Round tables fit better in smaller spaces than do square or rectangular ones. A small (about 4 feet in diameter) round table will comfortably seat four.

Window Dressings

Right: This kerchief-style window dressing embellished with a bead creates an interesting shape at the window. It filters out some light but doesn't block the view.

Below right: Curtains that cover just the bottom half of the window are a good option if you want to let the sunshine in but are concerned about privacy.

Below: A kitchen doesn't have to mean curtains. Venetian blinds—whether wood, metal, or plastic—can be used with great success in the kitchen as they are in other rooms in the house. They have clean lines and a classic look. A cautionary note: They can be tedious to clean.

Banks of cabinetry, long stretches of countertop, and boxy appliances combine to make your kitchen appear angular and sharp. Windows are the ideal place to break up straight lines, and to filter harsh light into a soft glow, with the visual and textural softness of fabric.

To choose fabric, study the rest of the materials used in the kitchen. Granite or solid-surfacing countertops, for instance, are often flecked with several colors. Pluck one of these hues for your window treatment. Patterned rugs and wallpaper also offer many color choices.

Whether you opt for a solid color or patterned window treatment depends on how much visual stimulation is going on in the rest of the room. If a granite, marble, or solid-surfacing countertop has an elaborate (if random) design, it can clash with a busy

curtain pattern, so stick to solid colors. If your backsplash has an intricate scheme, or if your cabinets are painted or stained with more than one shade, choose fabric with a simple, complementary pattern.

Remember, too, that some fabrics work better in the kitchen than others. If there's a sink nearby, don't go with a fabric that might stain or run if it's splashed with water or soapsuds (silk, for instance, is notorious for staining). If you'd like the treatment to block an unpleasant view, a dark or heavy fabric will do the trick. Lace or other loosely woven fabric such as gauze or scrim will obscure views but let in light. Never hang curtains above a cooktop or range.

Think, too, about the practical applications of your window's dressings. If blinding light beams through the window just as you're fixing dinner, you'll want to use a shade or heavier fabric but include a tieback for the curtains so you can enjoy the light when you're not standing by the window.

If you'd like some privacy while still basking in the sunshine, consider installing café curtains; they'll block the view from the

bottom half of the window but leave the top half clear. If privacy is not an issue and you're fortunate enough to have a great view of gardens or the backyard from the window, mount the treatment up and out of the way so that it's merely decorative.

Above: **Roman-style shades are a classic way to dress a window. Their lines are simple, yet the folds create a visual softness, and they can be raised or lowered to any height you desire.**
Left: **Incorporating a valance into your window dressing provides many options: The valance and curtains can be the same fabric, as shown here, or in different but coordinating fabrics. You might also consider a valance paired simply with a shade or a sheer curtain.**

Art and Accessories

Below: Take your family's refrigerator gallery to a new level: Frame a few pieces of your children's best artwork and display them with pride. They'll feel great, and your kitchen will look lovely.

A truly successful kitchen does more than function well; it has personality. Accessories, artwork, and treasures of all kinds are what gives a room its unique character. In composing the elements of a kitchen style, don't stop designing after the cabinets, countertops and appliances have been selected. Nudge your imagination into action, and treat your kitchen as an artist's canvas.

Don't banish artwork to more traditional display areas. Instead, look around your house for design ideas to bring into the kitchen. Framed prints can embellish carefully selected colors, fabrics, and surface materials throughout the kitchen. Small paintings might adorn a soffit. Larger pieces can enhance dining area walls. If framed prints seem too typical, consider a mural to spark conversation.

It's the little things that count

Often, it's the small touches that have the greatest effect on a decorating scheme. Because accessories are the most personal part of decorating, they should be chosen and displayed with care. Accent items should reflect your personality. Accessories don't have to be one-of-a-kind. If an item has meaning for you, it's worthy of attention.

Don't be shy about showing off your treasures. Beautiful dishes, mementos, heirlooms, or trinkets encourage guests to linger while the host cooks or cleans up.

Glass-front, china, and armoirelike cabinets are perfect for displaying collections. Unused space above cabinets also offer room for displays. Almost any collection can find a home in the kitchen. When arranging objects, keep scale and balance in mind, and don't overcrowd. To call attention to your collection, especially at night, consider spotlights or specially designed display lights.

Where to start

Go on a treasure hunt in your own house. Chances are, you'll come across an interesting object. Once you're sure you've unearthed all your house's hidden treasures, visit art galleries, antiques stores, and accessories shops. You'll develop a discerning eye.

Experiment with arrangements; rotate things into the kitchen from other rooms.

Vignettes are small scenes in a large setting, islands of beauty to behold. Countertops and other surfaces are candidates for a vignette. The idea is to create a composition that invites viewing and stirs interest, even if just in passing.

Above: There is much to look at—and love—in this kitchen that displays an affinity for folk art and country style: a collection of baskets handily hung from a pot rack, and display shelves decked out with Sunday paintings and bovine accessories.

Left: A collection of willow-ware and other blue-and-white china provides a bit of color in this neutral-toned kitchen. It also creates a visually pleasing and artful line along the soffit.

Get Kitchen Savvy

Welcome to Kitchen Design 101: Here's everything you need to know to create a floor plan you'll love.

Opposite: The mantra "location, location, location," applies to good kitchen design as well as real estate. This beautiful kitchen is a result of good planning with its ample counter space, use of natural materials laid out in a pleasing symmetry, and generous lanes around the island for ease of traffic flow.

There's a design maxim that says you have to know the rules before you can break them. This chapter is full of, if not rules, standards and guidelines for designing a kitchen. It also contains lots of good advice for working with a kitchen designer, and why it's a good idea, if it's within your budget to do so.

These standards and guidelines are the most recent put forth by the National Kitchen and Bath Association. Whether you're doing the design work yourself or hiring a designer, they will be enormously helpful in determining how your vision of a new kitchen can become a reality.

As in most disciplines, guidelines are established for a very good reason. Following them will give your kitchen nearly universal function and aesthetic appeal. That's not to say, however, that you can't break a rule or two and still wind up with an efficient and highly workable kitchen that looks great, too.

CONSIDER USING A FULL-SERVICE KITCHEN DESIGNER

Remodeling a kitchen is a complicated endeavor. For many homeowners, the cost of using a full-service designer is offset by avoiding costly mistakes, wasted time, and unsatisfactory results. Other advantages include:
- Professional measurements: The designer will ensure that the products ordered will fit your kitchen precisely.
- Design expertise: A designer has the experience and creativity to solve common design problems.
- Combined services: Designers make sure that everything is done correctly and on time.
- Professional drafting services: Clients can visualize the kitchen on paper and make changes in the early stages.
- Shopping services: Designers save homeowners time and frustration by suggesting appropriate products tailored to their style, budget, schedule, and construction preferences.

Kitchen Designers

Above: **The services of a kitchen designer range from creating a basic floor plan to helping you settle on a bold color scheme.** Below: **One advantage of hiring a kitchen designer is his or her ability to see storage potential in an odd sliver of space.**

If you're enlisting the services of a professional kitchen designer, the success of your new kitchen depends on the working relationship between you and the designer. Here's how to find the right person—and the right level of service—for the job.

The interview

While you are interviewing designers for the job, they are probably "interviewing" you, too, to determine whether they can meet your requirements and your budget.

If your initial discussions go well, a designer will likely conduct a more thorough survey of your needs, and your project will be underway. Be ready to answer or discuss these questions.

Are there other professionals involved in your project? It's common for homeowners to work with architects, interior designers, builders, and other professionals. The kitchen designer should contact them to open lines of communication. If you are not yet working with other professionals, the designer's firm may offer

any or all of these services, either with in-house personnel or through its network of construction and design professionals.

What kind of kitchen do you envision? Whether you're remodeling a kitchen or building a new home, the designer needs to know how much planning you've done, as well as style, color, and equipment preferences. Write down as much information as you can and take your list when you visit the designer. The more preliminary information you provide, the closer the designer can come to your dream kitchen.

When do you plan to start and complete your project? Scheduling sub-contractors is a key task in a building or remodeling project. Some cabinetry may be ready for immediate delivery from local warehouses, while custom or semicustom cabinets may require up to 16 weeks for delivery. The designer will help establish a schedule, then work to meet those deadlines.

What is your budget? The kitchen designer needs to know your budget constraints to help maximize your dollar, evaluate the cost-efficiency of products, and make effective trade-offs. A minor kitchen remodeling including new appliances could cost less than $10,000. A showcase kitchen or remodeling that involves major structural changes could exceed $50,000.

If you don't know how much to budget for your kitchen, start with these guidelines from the building and remodeling industry: If you're remodeling to put your house on the market, set a budget that's approximately 10 percent of the value of your home. If you intend to live in your home long-term, 25 percent is more realistic.

Designer services

Kitchen designers generally offer three levels of service, depending on the amount of help you want from them.

Level I—Basic Layout: Retailers such as lumberyards, home centers, and kitchen and bath distributors often offer computer-generated images of your new kitchen for free. You are responsible for providing accurate measurements as well as installation of cabinets, appliances, and surfacing materials. You probably will not receive much customization or problem-solving expertise.

Level II—Design Strategies: Many retailers employ designers who can discuss your remodeling needs and preferences and offer suggestions. The designer will visit your home to take measurements and later present a floor plan and ideas. After analyzing the plan, you may request changes.

The designer may or may not handle installation. This level of service usually involves a fee, either a minimal measurement fee or a design fee.

Level III—Design/Project Management: At the highest level of service, your designer will work with you to oversee the project from start to finish. He or she will analyze the kitchen and adjoining areas, look for potential structural changes, and create working drawings for your inspection. Once the plans are finalized, the full-service designer will order products and monitor the remodeling process.

This level is more typical of kitchen dealers, design firms, and remodelers.

Fee structures

Fees vary depending on location and the designer's level of expertise.

Some designers require a retainer or consultation fee on their initial visit. It is most commonly an hourly fee, but it may be a percentage of the project's total estimated cost. Typically, this fee is not applied toward the cost of any products you buy through the designer or the designer's employer.

Designers who sell products may include the design fee in the cost of the product. If you don't proceed with the project, you will probably be charged for designer services.

Preparing for your first visit

Before you meet with a designer, hone in on your style preferences by studying magazines, visiting with friends, and contemplating your family's lifestyle. Create a scrapbook of ideas by cutting out photos and circling the elements that catch your eye. Make notes about things you like and dislike, about the way your family lives in your kitchen and about suggestions you've received. Take these to your first meeting. The better prepared you are, the more likely it is you'll get exactly what you want. Here's an outline to get the ball rolling:

■ Major structural changes needed.
■ General style and color preferences.
■ Cabinetry—style, color, wood type, and organizational features, such as bins for flatware, and pullout shelves.
■ Appliances, sinks—style, color, functional features. Do you need a prep sink, or two ovens or dishwashers?

■ Surfacing materials for countertops, flooring, and backsplashes.
■ Number of cooks: What are the responsibilities of each? What appliances and equipment are required by each?
■ Workstations: Do you want auxiliary workstations, such as a baking center, laundry area, or homework space?
■ Planning area: How much desk space do you need? Do you want file drawers, bookshelves, or mail cubbies?
■ Eating area: Would you prefer a full eat-in kitchen, a breakfast nook, or a snack counter?
■ Social areas: Do you need seating for guests? A hospitality/beverage center, a TV area, or a snack station for children?

The lesson is a simple one: Know your priorities and limitations. That's the best way to ensure that a designer can deliver the kitchen you really want.

Above: A kitchen designer can help you make the visual transition from the kitchen to the rest of the living space—such as this open kitchen/family room arrangement—both practical and stylistically cohesive.

Kitchen Design Guidelines

Above: This geometrically themed kitchen showcases a stellar example of the tight, efficient work triangle—the distance between the primary cooktop, sink, and refrigerator. It's recommended this distance be no more than 26 feet, with no single leg of the triangle shorter than 4 feet and none longer than 9 feet.

These basic design standards are laid down by the National Kitchen and Bath Association. For more information about kitchen design, products, and other issues, or for even more specific design guidelines, contact the NKBA at 687 Willow Grove Street, Hackettstown, New Jersey, 07840. Phone: 877/NKBA-PRO (877/652-2776); or visit their website at www.nkba.org.

Guidelines for traffic & workflow

■ Doorways should be at least 32 inches wide and not more than 24 inches deep. When two counters flank a doorway entry, the minimum 32-inch-wide clearance should be allowed from the point of one counter to the closest point of the counter on the opposite side.

■ Walkways (passages between vertical objects greater than 24 inches deep where not more than one is a work counter or appliance) should be 36 inches wide.

■ Work aisles (passages between vertical objects, both of which are work counters or appliances) should be at least 42 inches wide in one-cook kitchens, at least 48 inches wide in multiple-cook kitchens.

■ The work triangle (the shortest walking distance between the refrigerator, sink, and

primary cooking surface) should be no more than 26 feet, with no single leg of the work triangle shorter than 4 feet nor longer than 9 feet. The work triangle should not intersect an island or peninsula by any more than 12 inches.

■ If two or more people cook at the same time, a work triangle should be placed for each cook. One leg of the primary and secondary triangles may be shared, but the two should not cross one another. Appliances may be shared or separate.

■ No major traffic patterns should cross through the work triangle.

■ No entry, appliance, or cabinet doors should interfere with another.

■ In a seating area, 36 inches of clearance should be allowed from the counter or table edge to any wall or obstruction behind it if no traffic will pass behind a seated diner. If there is a walkway behind the seating area, 65 inches of clearance, total, including the walkway, should be allowed between the seating area and any wall or obstruction.

Guidelines for cabinets & storage

Wall Cabinet Frontage: Small kitchens (less than 150 square feet): Allow at least 144 inches of wall cabinet frontage, with cabinets at least 12 inches deep and a minimum of 30 inches high (or equivalent) that feature adjustable shelving. Difficult-to-reach cabinets above the range hood, oven, or refrigerator do not count unless devices are installed within the case to improve accessibility.

Large kitchens (more than 150 square feet): Allow at least 186 inches of wall cabinet frontage, with cabinets at least 12 inches deep, and a minimum of 30 inches high (or equivalent) which feature adjustable shelving. Difficult-to-reach cabinets above the range hood, oven, or refrigerator do not count unless devices are installed within the case to improve accessibility.

■ In either small or large kitchens, diagonal or pie-cut wall cabinets count as a total of 24 inches.

■ Cabinets 72 inches or taller can count as

either base cabinets or wall cabinets, but not both. The calculation is as follows:

- 12-inch-deep, tall units = 1x the base lineal footage, 2x the wall lineal footage.
- 18-inch-deep, tall units = 1.5x the base lineal footage, 3x the wall lineal footage.
- 21- to 24-inch-deep, tall units = 2x the base lineal footage, 4x the wall lineal footage.
- At least 60 inches of wall cabinet frontage, with cabinets at least 12 inches deep, a minimum of 30 inches high (or equivalent) should be included within 72 inches of the primary sink centerline.

Base Cabinet Frontage: Small kitchens (less than 150 square feet): Allow at least 156 inches of base cabinet frontage, with cabinets at least 21 inches deep (or equivalent).

Large kitchens (more than 150 square feet): Allow at least 192 inches of base cabinet frontage, with cabinets at least 21 inches deep (or equivalent).

- In both small and large kitchens, pie-cut or lazy Susan base cabinets count as a total of 30 inches.
- Cabinets 72 inches or taller can count as either base or wall cabinets, but not both. The calculation is as follows:
- 12-inch-deep, tall units = 1x the base lineal footage, 2x the wall lineal footage.
- 18-inch-deep, tall units = 1.5x the base lineal footage, 3x the wall lineal footage.
- 21- to 24-inch-deep, tall units = 2x the base lineal footage, 4x the wall lineal footage.

Drawer/Roll-out Shelf Frontage: Small kitchens (less than 150 square feet): Allow at least 120 inches of drawer or roll-out shelf frontage.

Large kitchens (more than 150 square feet): Allow at least 165 inches of drawer or roll-out shelf frontage.

- Multiply the cabinet width by the number of drawers and roll-outs to determine the frontage. Drawers or roll-out cabinets must be at least 15 inches wide and 21 inches deep to be counted.
- At least five storage or organizing items, located between 15 and 48 inches above the finished floor (or extending into that area) should be included in the kitchen to improve functionality and accessibility. These items may include but are not limited to lowered wall cabinets; raised base cabinets; tall cabinets; appliance garages, bins and racks/swing-out pantries; interior vertical dividers; and specialized drawers and shelves. Full-extension drawers and roll-out shelves greater than the 120-inch minimum for small kitchens or 165 inches for larger kitchens may also be included.
- For kitchens with usable corner areas in the plan, at least one functional corner storage unit should be included.
- The top edge of a waste receptacle should be no higher than 36 inches. The receptacle should be easily accessible and should be removable without raising the receptacle bottom higher than the unit's physical height. Lateral removal of the receptacle which does not require lifting is preferred.

Guidelines for counter surface & landing space

At least two work-counter heights should be installed in the kitchen for different uses and functions, with one between 28 and 36 inches above the finished floor and the other 36 to 45 inches above the finished floor.

Countertop Frontage: Small kitchens (less than 150 square feet): Allow at least 132 inches of usable countertop frontage.

Above: **When planning for a full-height cabinet (one that goes to or almost to the ceiling), determine what the maximum reach of the primary user will be. Take into account the cabinet's depth to allow at least 36 inches of clearance for bending between the cabinet and another object. If you hang a pot rack, be sure the pots don't interfere with normal cooking or food preparation.**
Left: **A short stretch of countertop allows for a secondary sink. The depth of a countertop should be no less than 16 inches.**

Above: This kitchen beautifully adheres to the guideline for at least two work-counter heights of different materials to assist with a variety of kitchen tasks. The butcher block is great for chopping vegetables; the granite just right for rolling dough or setting down a hot pot. One surface should be between 28 and 36 inches above the floor; the other should be 36 to 45 inches above the floor.

Large kitchens (more than 150 square feet): Allow at least 198 inches of usable countertop frontage.

■ Counters must be a minimum of 16 inches deep, and wall cabinets must be at least 15 inches above their surface for the counter to be included in the total frontage measurement. Measure only countertop frontage; do not count corner space.

■ If an appliance garage or storage cabinet extends to the counter, there must be 16 inches of clear space in front of this cabinet for the area to be counted as usable countertop frontage.

■ There should be at least 24 inches of countertop frontage to one side of the primary sink and 18 inches on the other side (including corner sink applications), with the 24-inch counter frontage at the same counter height as the sink. Countertop frontage may be a continuous surface or the total of two angled countertop sections. Measure only countertop frontage; do not count corner space.

■ The minimum allowable space from a corner to the edge of the primary sink is 3 inches; it should also be a minimum of 15 inches from that corner to the sink centerline.

■ If there is anything less than 18 inches of frontage from the edge of the primary sink to a corner, 21 inches of clear counter (measure frontage) should be allowed on the return.

■ At least 3 inches of countertop frontage should be provided on one side of secondary sinks and 18 inches on the other side (including corner sink applications), with

the 18-inch counter frontage at the same counter height as the sink. The countertop frontage may be a continuous surface or the total of two angled countertop sections. Measure only countertop frontage; do not count corner space.

■ At least 15 inches of landing space, a minimum of 16 inches deep, should be planned above, below, or adjacent to a microwave oven.

■ In an open-ended kitchen configuration, at least 9 inches of counter space should be allowed on one side of the cooking surface and 15 inches on the other, at the same counter height as the appliance. For an enclosed configuration, at least 3 inches of clearance space should be planned at an end wall protected by flame-retardant surfacing material and 15 inches should be allowed on the other side of the appliance, at the same counter height as the appliance.

■ For safety reasons, countertop should also extend a minimum of 9 inches behind the cooking surface, at the same counter height as the appliance, in any instance where there is not an abutting wall or backsplash.

■ In an outside-angle installation of cooking surfaces, there should be at least 9 inches of straight counter space on one side and 15 inches of straight counter space on the other side, at the same counter height as the appliance.

■ Allow for at least 15 inches counter space on the latch side of the refrigerator or on either side of a side-by-side refrigerator; or, at least 15 inches of landing space that is no more than 48 inches across from the refrigerator.

■ Although it is not ideal, it is acceptable to place an oven adjacent to a refrigerator. For convenience, the refrigerator should be the appliance placed next to the available countertop. If there is no safe landing area across from the oven, this arrangement may be reversed.

■ Allow for at least 15 inches of landing space that is at least 16 inches deep next to or above the oven if the appliance door opens into a primary traffic pattern. At least 15 x 16 inches of landing space that is no more than 48 inches across from the oven is acceptable if the appliance does not open into a traffic area.

■ Plan for at least 36 inches of continuous

countertop that is at least 16 inches deep for the preparation center. The preparation center should be immediately adjacent to a water source.

■ The preparation center can be placed between the primary sink and the cooking surface, between the refrigerator and the primary sink, or adjacent to a secondary sink on an island or other cabinet section.

■ No two primary work centers (the main sink, refrigerator, preparation, or cooktop/range center) should be separated by a full-height, full-depth tall tower, such as an oven cabinet, pantry cabinet, or refrigerator.

■ Countertop corners should be clipped or curved; counter edges should be eased to eliminate sharp corners.

Guidelines for appliance placement & use/clearance space

■ Knee space, which may be open or adaptable, should be planned below or adjacent to sinks, cooktops, ranges, and ovens whenever possible. Knee space should be a minimum of 27 inches high by 30 inches wide by 19 inches deep under the counter. The 27-inch height may decrease progressively as depth increases. Surfaces in the knee space area should be finished for safety and aesthetic purposes.

■ Allow for a clear floor space of 30 x 48 inches at the sink, dishwasher, cooktop, oven, and refrigerator. These spaces may overlap, and up to 19 inches of knee space beneath an appliance, counter cabinet, etc., may be part of the total 30-inch and/or 48-inch dimension.

■ Allow for a minimum of 21 inches of clear floor space between the edge of the dishwasher and counters, appliances, and/or cabinets that are placed at a right angle to the dishwasher.

■ The edge of the primary dishwasher should be within 36 inches of the edge of one sink. The dishwasher should be accessible to more than one person at a time to accommodate other cooks, kitchen clean-up helpers, and/or other family members.

■ If the kitchen has only one sink, it should be located between or across from the cooking surface, preparation area, or refrigerator.

■ Allow at least 24 inches of clearance between the cooking surface and a protected surface above, or at least 30 inches of clearance between the cooking surface and an unprotected surface above. If the protected surface is a microwave hood combination, manufacturer's specifications may dictate a smaller clearance.

■ All major appliances used for surface cooking should have a ventilation system, with a fan rated at 150 cubic feet of air per minute minimum.

■ Do not place the cooking surface below an operable window unless the window is 3 inches or more behind the appliance and more than 24 inches above it. Windows, operable or inoperative, above a cooking surface should not be dressed with flammable window treatments.

■ Place the microwave oven so the bottom of the appliance is between 24 and 48 inches above the floor.

Below: A narrow granite-topped island provides a comfortable dining spot in the kitchen while still allowing for the 36-inch-wide aisle recommended for easy traffic flow.

Plumbing and Electrical Issues

As fun as it is to contemplate having beautiful cabinetry and countertops and gleaming faucets and flooring, the least glamorous of kitchen-remodeling decisions need to be made first: Evaluate your home's plumbing and electrical systems and plan for adding or changing them to accommodate the new elements.

Plumbing

If you're gutting the space and starting over, save money by leaving plumbing lines where they are; but if you're moving the sink or adding one, both water pipes and drains will have to be moved.

Perhaps the biggest plumbing issue in kitchen remodeling (especially if you're rearranging the elements of your kitchen) is how far the sink trap can stray from the vertical stack—also called a soil stack. The sink trap is a curved section of drain pipe

Below: One plumbing decision you'll have to make in a kitchen remodel is whether to install a water filtration system. This version attaches at the faucet; there are others that are installed under the sink.

that holds enough standing water to make an airtight seal, which prevents sewer gases from backing up and leaking into your home. The stack is the typically 4-inch, fixed pipe that all of the usually 1½-inch sink pipes in the home flow into; it takes liquid and solid waste out of the house and into the sewer or septic system.

Local plumbing codes require that a sink trap must be located within a specified distance of the stack. Your plumber will have to install your sink so that it is in compliance with local code.

Electrical

If you're enlarging the size of your kitchen or adding features, you'll need to increase the amount of amperage allotted to the space. If you own an older home, you may already be aware of this—if, for instance, you have inconveniently blown a fuse when the toaster and microwave were being used at the same time.

With a kitchen plan in hand, sit down with your contractor and/or electrician and go over locations for each electrical outlet and telephone and television jack you plan to have in your kitchen.

Some appliances and electrical systems require special considerations, and some of the heaviest hitters in the wattage-requirement department are used in the kitchen: the refrigerator, microwave, and toaster, for instance. A floor-warming system—often installed under ceramic tile to take the chill off its surface—may require its own circuit, and a stove or an electric dryer requires its own 240-volt circuit. Additionally, be sure ground fault circuit interrupters (GFCI) are specified for all electrical outlets.

If you're planning an Internet-accessible computer in the kitchen, plan for that, too, whether you hook up to the Web through a phone line, DSL, or cable modem.

You'll need to determine the sites of electrical outlets before wall tiles or backsplashes are installed. Remember that electrical equipment such as toasters and mixers should be used far from open flames or the heat of the stove; they also should be used nowhere near running water. Be sure to discuss these issues with the electrician who will be doing the wiring in your kitchen.

Ideally, electrical sockets should be situated near the cabinets where small appliances are stored and over the countertop or

Left: Special situations—such as incorporating a washer/dryer into your kitchen—require more-than-standard solutions. An electric dryer, for instance, requires its own 240 volt circuit.

Below left: If you're planning on having a computer with Internet access in your kitchen, you'll need to discuss the exact location of that with your electrician so the proper wiring and cable installation can be done.

other work surfaces where they are usually used so that you don't have to lift and haul hand mixers, bread machines, and food processors across the kitchen. Electrical outlets should also be placed at a height that allows the appliances to be easily used without the cord snaking around and cluttering the countertop.

If possible, have your electrician place the sockets at such a height that the cord lengths on your small appliances such as toasters and coffeemakers can be shortened, making them tidy and efficient to use.

HOW MANY OUTLETS DO I NEED?

The number of electrical outlets you need will depend somewhat on the size of your kitchen, of course, but generally, a well-outfitted kitchen requires up to seven individual circuits: a 120/240-volt circuit for an electric range; two separate 120-volt circuits for the dishwasher and microwave; at least two 120-volt small-appliance circuits above the countertop; and one general lighting circuit to supply all of the lights with electricity.

Countertop outlets can be no more than 4 feet apart so that, measuring horizontally, no point on the counter is more than 24 inches from an outlet.

Right: A microwave that is installed at this level—rather than over the cooktop or in an upper wall cabinet—is accessible to everyone, including people who use wheelchairs and children who are old enough to prepare their own microwavable snacks.

Universal Design

In most homes, the kitchen harbors irritating barriers for anyone in a wheelchair or impaired by other physical limitations. Cabinets and appliances are out of reach. Oven doors drop open and block access to the racks. Countertops are too high. And appliance knobs and faucets can be difficult to operate.

In the past decade, considerable research has been conducted to find ways to make life in the kitchen easier for people with disabilities. Because it is such a complex room, manufacturers of cabinetry, appliances, and plumbing fixtures have teamed with organizations such as the Center for Universal Design and the Paralyzed Veterans of America to find ways

to make tasks more comfortable, more convenient, and safer. Here are some ways they've discovered to make your kitchen more user-friendly.

Cabinetry and countertops

■ Take advantage of the specialty fittings that cabinetry manufacturers offer. Lazy Susans and pullout shelves bring cabinet contents into view and within reach. Pullout cutting boards can be removed and set on the lap of a seated cook.

■ If possible, install cabinet doors that slide horizontally, rather than pivoting outward.

■ Choose wide pulls rather than knobs to help people with hand-strength or dexterity problems.

■ Install a continuous line of countertop—absent of any obstructions—from the refrigerator to the sink to the cooktop to allow the cook to slide mixing and cooking vessels from one workstation to another.

■ Plan for at least 1½ feet of countertop adjacent to the refrigerator. This surface should be on the opening side of the fridge. If possible, the cooktop and oven should have about 2 feet of clear countertop surface on each side, so hot dishes can be set down. A right-handed cook needs 3 feet of work surface to the right of the sink and 2 feet of work space to the left.

■ Leave plenty of knee space under countertops to accommodate wheelchair users. The minimum measurements for knee space are 30 inches wide, 19 inches deep, and 27 inches high.

■ Keep most countertops at the standard height. To accommodate a person in a wheelchair, consider lowering one section of countertop, perhaps a peninsula or island. Alternatively, equip the kitchen with a cart that's a convenient height for a seated cook. Adjustable countertops are available on the market, but they are costly. The electronic systems can be raised and lowered to fit the height of each cook in the family.

Appliances and sinks

■ Choose a side-by-side refrigerator model to give a seated cook easy access. Models with ice and water dispensers in the door are especially convenient.

■ Plan for a separate cooktop and built-in wall oven. The cooktop can be installed at any height and knee space can be provided beneath it. Smooth glass-top models let the cook easily slide pots and pans. Choose a model with controls at the front so the

cook doesn't have to reach across burners. Built-in ovens also can be installed at the most convenient height. Be sure there is a landing space for hot pans and casseroles directly beside or in front of the oven.

■ Select a basin that is shallow and has the drain at the back to allow adequate knee space below. The area beneath the basin should be insulated to protect legs and feet from contact with hot and cold water pipes.

■ Provide easy control of water temperature and flow with lever-handle faucets. A gooseneck faucet or one with a retractable or pullout spray head eases filling tall pots.

For more information about designing a barrier-free kitchen, contact the National Kitchen and Bath Association, 687 Willow Grove St., Hackettstown, NJ 07840; Phone 877/652-2776; or The Center for Universal Design, North Carolina State University, P.O. Box 8613, Raleigh, NC 27695-8613; Phone 800/647-6777; Internet address: www2.ncsu.edu/ncsu/design/cud.

Above: **Electric glass cooktops with front-mounted controls add convenience and safety to a barrier-free kitchen. A person with limited strength or mobility can slide pans across the surface of the cooktop. The accessible front controls mean the cook doesn't have to reach across a hot surface.**

Far left: **Tall people or those with back problems love this idea: The dishwasher is raised a few inches to minimize bending. Also, the adjacent undersink cabinet is unencumbered by a cabinet floor, allowing a wheelchair to roll into the space. Here, totable wire racks are stored in the sink cabinet.** Left: **Removing hot food from a built-in oven is easier if the door is hinged on the side. One cautionary note: The side-opening door doesn't catch hot spills as a flat door does.**

Sketching Your Kitchen

And now, finally, it's time to bring your notes, doodles, and dreams to life—but first on paper.

Opposite: When you walk through the door each night and head to the kitchen to cook dinner, think of the satisfaction you'll feel in knowing you helped create a space that's beautiful, efficient, and just right for you.

There comes a point when all your kitchen dreams and ideas will need to be worked into a plan to be brought to life. No doubt you've been jotting lists, collecting pictures of things you like, and doodling ideas of what your kitchen might look like. So whether you'll be doing the design or will be working with a pro, this chapter will show you how the planning process works.

It's at this point—when ideas are committed to the space available—that many design issues come into closer view. If you need a full-strength ventilation hood to support the range you pine for, now's the time to make sure that it can actually be vented through your home. Opportunities for more items from your "want" list may appear. You may find that the offerings from a quality stock-cabinetry line will meet your needs, as opposed to the custom cabinetry you'd assumed necessary.

Whether you take the planning and design process from start to finish or invite a pro to help you, a full understanding of the planning process will reap a better finished kitchen. Turn the page to see how it works.

Planning Space

MEASURING TOOLS

Blast through the measuring task
with the right tools at hand:

- 25-foot steel tape measure
- Sharp pencil
- ¼-inch graph paper
- A few sheets of tracing paper
- A good quality artist's eraser
- 12-inch architect's
combination ruler and scale

Right: To make it function
well, a large kitchen with
(seemingly) room to spare
requires careful measuring
and planning as much as a
small kitchen does.

Below: Though a tiny
kitchen may be more of a
design challenge than a
large one, it's particularly
satisfying to create a
small but super-efficient
space such as this.

Your Dream Kitchen on Paper

Your successful kitchen remodeling
starts with a clear picture of the
space available to you—the dimensions of your blank canvas. To get at this
canvas, forget about existing cabinets, counters, appliances, and other components.
Simply imagine an empty room— nothing
but walls, windows, floor, and ceiling.

You'll need to measure your kitchen
space in order to get the best picture of what
you have to work with. That means carefully measuring the space and drawing it into
an accurate, scaled floor plan. Do you have
the original blueprints of your house? If so,
you have a jump start on the measuring project, but you'll still have to check the plans
against the room's actual dimensions to
make sure the room was built as planned.
Measuring can also reveal flaws—walls not
plumb, corners not square, floors not level—
that can affect both the final cabinet dimensions and how the cabinets are installed.

Whether you or your design professional take the measurements, here's how to get started. Choose a steel measuring tape, preferably 25 feet long, over a yardstick or cloth tape. Record measurements in inches and feet. You'll use both measurements in the process. Cabinets and appliances, for example, are measured in inches.

Measuring your space

1. Carefully measure the perimeter dimensions of the room. Next, draw an outline of the space on ¼-inch graph paper. Use a scale of ¼ inch per foot. Using a ruler and triangle will help you keep lines straight and corners perpendicular.

2. Measure and label the room's more detailed dimensions. Start in a corner and work your way around the room in one direction. Place the tape against the wall, 36 inches from the floor, and measure from corner to trim edge of the nearest doorway or window. Note the measurement to the nearest ¹⁄₁₆ inch. Be sure to measure the width of the trim, too.

3. Measure and note the location and width of each doorway and window (the space between the inside edges of the trim). Also note the hinging and swing of each door and to which side of the space it extends.

4. Measure from the floor to the bottom edge of the trim under the windowsill. For any window that is over a counter, the distance between the sill and the countertop will be the height of the backsplash area.

5. Measure the height of the room from floor to ceiling. Take this measurement in all corners and at midpoints in each wall, checking to see if the floor is level. Note any discrepancies.

6. With the help of a partner, measure from a couple of points along a wall to the same points on the opposite wall (again, 36 inches from the floor). Doing so will reveal if either wall is bowed in or out. If possible, take diagonal, corner-to-corner measurements to see if the room is evenly squared. If the two diagonal measurements are not the same in a rectangular or square room, find out the degree of error in each corner by using the 3-4-5 right triangle method: Measure 3 feet out from the corner on one

wall and 4 feet out on the other. If the corner is square, the distance between these two points will be exactly 5 feet. If it's more or less, determine the extent of the error on the "short" wall, that is, the one where a cabinet run terminates or has the shorter of the two runs to that corner. Adjusting the cabinets on the shorter length will require less effort.

7. Measure and note the exact locations and dimensions of radiators, registers, switches, receptacles, light fixtures, and, if possible, places where plumbing and gas connections come through the wall or floor.

Below: **When taking your measurements, it's a good idea also to measure the dimensions of the space adjacent to your kitchen, should you decide to annex all or some of it, as was done with this remodeled kitchen.**

8. When you finish a wall, add up the individual measurements and check the total against your original measurement of the entire wall. If there's any difference, start over.

9. Measure all the other walls in the same manner to complete your sketch of the room with all necessary measurements and details.

10. Measure each wall and draw detailed elevation views (including doorways, windows, and permanent fixtures), like the wall view. When complete, the sketch of your space should resemble the floor plans in this chapter.

Dreaming and Drawing

Now you're ready to work with the layout and make rough sketches of optional floor plans. After you've drawn an accurate floor plan, you and/or your design pro can use it as a guide for sketching ideas. Lay tracing paper over the drawing and sketch in various layouts.

Maybe that U-shape kitchen has room for an island. Perhaps a peninsula could turn your L-shape kitchen into a full or partial U. Who knows?

As you develop favorite arrangements, you'll want to become familiar with standard appliance and cabinetry dimensions. Check your plans against recommended guidelines listed in Kitchen Design Guidelines, pages 90–93. And if you want to change the location of a sink or a fixed electrical or gas appliance, put in a call to your local government to ensure that you'll be complying with building code. It's much easier and cheaper to change plans now rather than later.

Laying out cabinets

Your choices in kitchen cabinetry may seem endless, but cabinet sizes are fairly standardized. Standard sizing is helpful in that most fixtures and appliances have been sized to coordinate with standard cabinet dimensions. All stock, ready-to-assemble (RTA), and the majority of semicustom and custom cabinetry lines conform to these standards. You can buy or build cabinetry to nonstandard dimensions if needed, of course.

If ready-made cabinets are your choice, you'll find that base and wall cabinets come in widths that vary in 3-inch increments, typically from 9 to 48 inches. Filler strips that match the cabinet finish fill gaps that inevitably occur between corner walls and the end of a cabinet run.

Base cabinets

Base cabinets are 24 inches deep and 34½ inches high (with a 1½-inch counter on top, the cabinet height reaches the standard 36 inches). Keep in mind that base cabinets less than 15 inches wide are useful for little other than vertical tray storage, so choose the number of narrow units carefully.

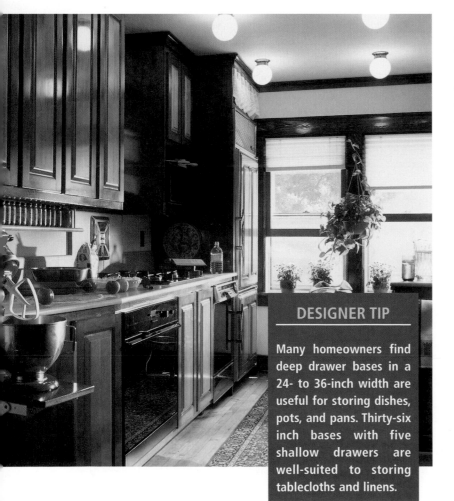

DESIGNER TIP

Many homeowners find deep drawer bases in a 24- to 36-inch width are useful for storing dishes, pots, and pans. Thirty-six inch bases with five shallow drawers are well-suited to storing tablecloths and linens.

Wall cabinets

Most wall cabinets are 12 to 13 inches deep and 30 to 42 inches high. Thirty-six inches is a popular height in a kitchen with an 8-foot ceiling, leaving room for either a soffit or an open space between the cabinet and ceiling. However, installing a 36-inch wall cabinet, running right up to the top of an 8-foot ceiling, makes room for an additional shelf inside.

Refrigerator cabinets

Refrigerator cabinets are a dimensional cross between wall and base cabinets. The actual cabinet portion is mounted over the top of the refrigerator, and is as deep as the appliance. These cabinets generally measure 36 inches wide and 18 inches high. If you'll be ordering a refrigerator cabinet, installing the cabinet with a rollout storage fitting will make the deep space far more accessible.

Pantry cabinets

Thanks to the many pullout storage fittings available, a high-capacity pantry can be had in just a sliver of space. Pantry cabinet widths range in 3-inch increments from 15 to 36 inches. Most, up to 30 inches wide, stand 84 inches high. Thirty-six-inch pantries generally stand 90 inches high, and 42-inch pantries, 96 inches high. Most pantry cabinets are available with shelves or fold-out chef's pantry fittings—or can be left open to serve as a broom/utility closet.

Left: A narrow cabinet fitted with several full-extension drawers allows you to organize lots of little things—and get to them easily.
Below: Exceedingly careful measurements assure that the drawer in this base cabinet doesn't collide with the knobs on the cooktop when the drawer is pulled out.

FINE-TUNING YOUR CABINET FACES

At this point, the biggest variable is cabinet configurations. Here are some tips for fine-tuning your cabinet faces.

• Base cabinets up to 21 inches wide generally carry one door or single bank of drawers. Doors shouldn't be any wider or they'll swing too far out into the kitchen. Drawer cabinets can be much wider, up to 36 inches.

• Stock and ready-to-assemble wall cabinets can be up to 21 inches wide in a single-door style, but it's a good idea to keep them at 18 inches or less. The main drawback to a wider door is that when it swings out it is awkward looking and can hurt someone who stands up beneath the open door.

• Avoid colliding open drawers by keeping drawer cabinets away from inside corners in your kitchen.

• For an orderly appearance, keep doors and drawers in vertical and horizontal alignment.

Hardworking Centers

casserole dishes, cookbooks, and small appliances. A pantry with roll-out shelving makes reaching that can of soup in the back of the cupboard a snap.

Situate the primary food storage near the longest stretch of countertop for easy access to items while cooking. The best places for food storage are those cabinets attached to cool outside walls near shaded north-facing windows, if possible. Cabinets and walls near heat sources—such as the dishwasher, oven, or refrigerator—are not ideal places for storing foods.

Consider a snack center, which might have a small microwave, a wrapping station for lunches and leftovers, a small refrigerator or cooling drawer, and even a second sink. Putting one section of countertop lower than the rest creates a place for kids to make their own snacks.

Place the latch side of the refrigerator facing into the work triangle. The door should open completely so the bins can be pulled out easily. The refrigerator door should not swing into a doorway.

Food Storage and Prep

Above: A built-in cutting board situated right above handy pull-out storage for foodstuffs makes food prep a snap.
Top: Fresh foods that don't need to be refrigerated, such as onions, can be kept in a cool, dry place or displayed in a basket on the counter.
Right: It's easier to lift appliances from below onto the counter than it is to climb up a stepstool to retrieve them from above.

As the kitchen's work triangle has three points—the cooktop or range, sink, and refrigerator—the kitchen itself has three work centers: food storage and preparation, cooking, and cleanup. Here are some points about each to keep in mind when designing your new kitchen.

Although many busy families eat reheated takeout food or preprepared meals from the grocery store more often than dinner all-from-scratch, it's still important to have ample food storage and preparation space. This work center should be equipped for weekend cooks who enjoy making a big meal.

Be sure to plan well-organized storage for canned and dry goods, mixing bowls,

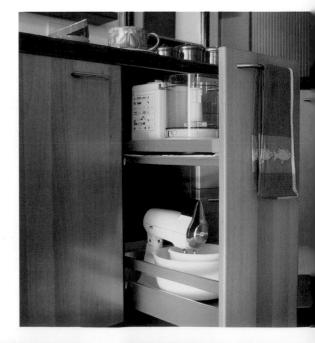

Above: If you're an avid baker, consider a subcategory of the food storage and preparation center: a baking center. The countertop can be cool and smooth marble for rolling out dough, and the center can be equipped with clever storage such as the tucked-away "closet" housing the food processor in this kitchen.

A large expanse of countertop is surrounded on both sides with food storage for fresh food as well as canned and dry goods. Mixing bowls, spoons, spatulas, and cookbooks are right at the cook's fingertips.

Hanging cooking implements such as pots, pans, and colanders right above the cooktop where they're used saves time, energy, and steps.

Cooking

The main ingredients of the cooking center are the cooktop or range and the microwave oven. Be sure your cooking center has ample storage for all the tools of the cooking trade: pots and pans, utensils, pot holders, hot pads, spices and seasonings, and food products that go directly from the storage container into the simmering pot.

A cooktop is safest and most efficient with at least 18 inches of counter space on each side. This enables you to turn handles away from traffic and provides a landing space for hot pots. Use a heat-resistant countertop surface around the cooktop or range.

Whether you have a cooktop or a range, the cooking center always requires a ventilation system. The number of Btus put off by your cooktop will determine the requirement of your ventilation system. A standard four-burner residential range requires a ventilation system that blows a minimum of 150 cubic feet of air per minute. Professional-style cooktops and ranges require more ventilation. See page 60 for more information on ventilation systems.

Above: Everything a serious cook needs to whisk a hollandaise, strain a broth, or ladle a soup is in full view and can be in hand in seconds.

Both the cooktop and microwave are integrated into the cooking center. Extra-wide drawers and pull-out shelving hold pots and pans. Dishes are stored in a cabinet above a run of countertop within a few easy steps of the cooktop to make serving a breeze.

Cleanup

The sink is the centerpiece of the cleanup center. It also is an integral element of the food preparation and cooking centers. Locate the sink at the center of the work triangle, between the range and refrigerator.

The other primary components of the cleanup center are the garbage disposal and dishwasher, so dirty plates can be scraped and loaded into the dishwasher with no wasted steps. The dishwasher should be placed right next to the sink to minimize drips on the floor. It should be to the left of the sink if the main cook is right-handed,

and to the right if that person is left-handed.

You can store your everyday dishes, glassware, and utensils near the dishwasher for easy unloading, but you may prefer another convenient location, such as near the dining table.

If your plans include a trash compactor, have it installed on the side of the sink opposite the dishwasher. This saves steps and makes effective use of the countertop.

The cleanup center also requires ample storage for dish towels, cleaning products, and a garbage can. It's also an idea spot for a recycling system.

Right: A dishrack built into a corner above the sink saves counter space in the cleanup center and keeps drips on the floor and countertop at a minimum.

Above: **Open shelving above the sink for storage of pans and dishware makes washing, drying, and putting away a one-position proposition.**

The sink and dishwasher are situated handily right below the primary dinnerware storage area in this kitchen. Cleaning products are stored in a cabinet right under the sink. If you have small children, be sure the door can be locked. A trash receptacle/recycling bin is neatly hidden in a pullout, so scraping plates, rinsing them, and loading them in the dishwasher can be done in one fell swoop.

Elevations and Floor Plans Defined

When you or your kitchen design pro completes a basic kitchen design that you like, then it's time for a final floor plan that includes the position of all your cabinets, appliances, features and utility connections. A well-marked plan will go a long way in preventing time- and money-consuming changes during the actual remodeling process.

A floor plan is the overhead view of an architectural plan, what you'd see if you lifted the roof and looked down on the space.

An elevation view is the wall view of a space, what you'd see—from floor to ceiling—if you stood across from a wall.

An overhead or floor plan view gives you a good idea how a layout occupies space. An elevation view lets you see how the kitchen is going to look to the human eye—the arrangements of doors and drawers, how wall and base cabinets relate to each other, how appliances function in a work triangle. An elevation takes in one wall at a time and—like the plan view—shows the cabinets, appliances, fixtures, and outlets.

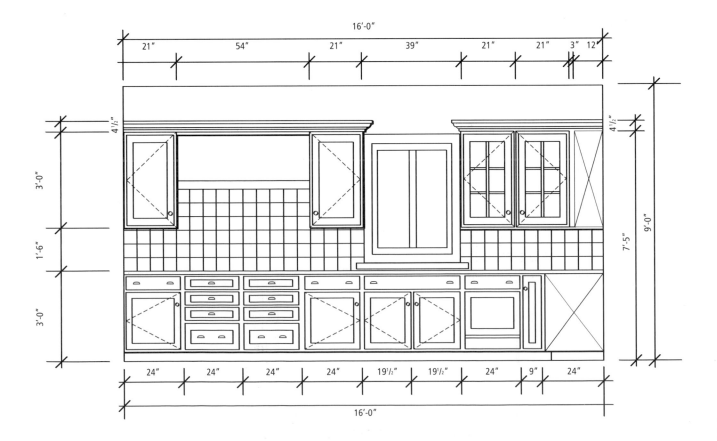

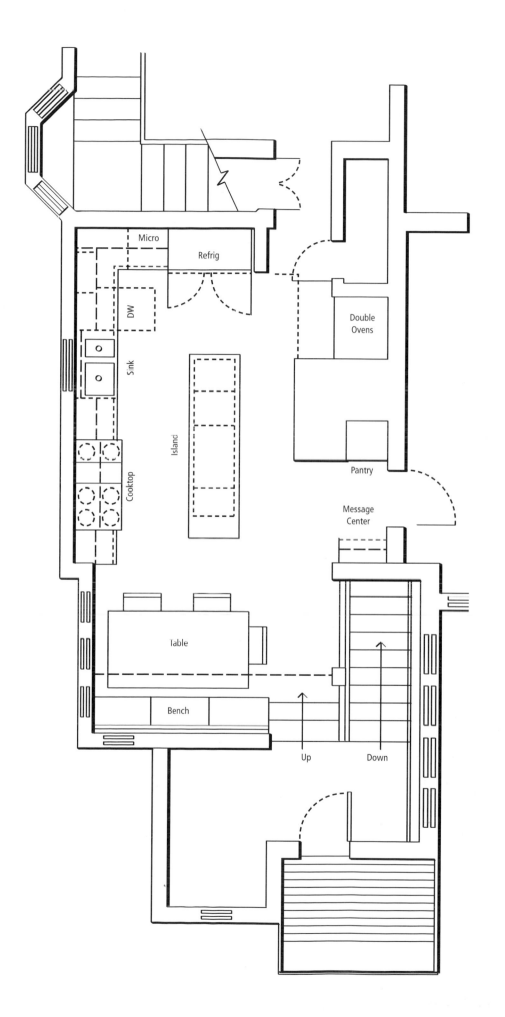

Labels on floor plan: Micro, Refrig, DW, Sink, Cooktop, Island, Double Ovens, Pantry, Message Center, Table, Bench, Up, Down

Left: A floor plan gives you a bird's-eye view of all of the major elements in the kitchen: walls; windows; major appliances such as the cooktop, sink, and refrigerator; closets; dining areas; and both wall and base cabinets. Base cabinets and countertops are represented by a solid line around the perimeter of the room, wall cabinets by a dotted line.

Two Kitchens, One Budget

Certain criteria are common to most kitchen remodels. They are:

■ Get the most for your money.
■ Make the space the most efficient it can be.
■ Make zones for each task and incorporate "point of use" storage.
■ Make maintenance easy.
■ Create a kitchen that reflects your personality and desires.
■ Maximize functional and beauty.

Beyond that, every person has different priorities for his or her kitchen. One may want an aesthetically perfect space to blend seamlessly with the rest of the house—but may not cook much in it. Another may be an avid cook and baker, so may want the best appliances the budget allows. Every remodeling pie gets divided and enjoyed very differently. Consequently, each remodeling job requires that compromises and choices be made so the homeowner gets the kitchen that best reflects who he or she is and how the kitchen will be used.

To show how one remodeling budget can be spent very differently depending on a family's needs and desires, we took a hypothetical $35,000 and gave it to two hypothetical families to "spend" on a new kitchen that suited their needs, assuming they both started with the same outdated kitchen. Here's how they turned out:

Family A

Family B

Above and Right: Two very different kitchens can be built into the same space for the same money depending on the needs and desires of the people who will be cooking, eating, and living there. When making your own kitchen plan, make a list of your requirement, and plan for those first, before adding luxuries.

Family A (Father, mother, two young children)

Requirements:

- Lots of countertop area to make family meals
- Informal buffet serving area
- Large refrigerator
- Backyard view to watch children at play
- Kitchen open to family room
- Countertop seating for four
- Pantry storage
- Trash compactor
- Durable countertop surfaces
- Bulletin board for children's schedules and artwork
- Message center with phone
- Cookbook storage
- High-quality cabinets to make every inch of space hardworking

How their budget was spent:

Cabinetry: Custom raised panel $16,000
Countertop: Granite with decorative edge . . . . $ 5,000
Appliances: Standard grade . . . . $ 3,800
Sink, faucet, lights: Standard grade . . . . $ 3,000
Flooring, wall finishes: Hardwood/paint . . . . $ 3,000
Construction and Installation: Add pass-through opening, install . . . . . $ 4,200
$35,000

Above: A peninsula in the family kitchen serves as both a dining area for casual meals and an informal buffet serving area for parties. It also provides additional seating for the adjacent family room.

Family B (Empty-nesters, with four grown children and grandchildren)

Requirements:

- Intimate seating for two
- Ample seating for when family comes to visit
- Upscale, easily operated appliances
- Gourmet coffee maker
- Open feel for informal entertaining
- Glass doors to display collectibles
- Areas for two cooks to work at the same time
- Uncluttered, organized, sleek look
- Low-maintenance
- Television with DVD/CD player
- Place to grow plants

How their budget was spent:

Cabinetry: Stock, with stained recessed panels . . . . $ 9,000
Countertops: Bevel-edge laminate . . . . $ 2,000
Appliances: Upgrade . . . . $ 9,500
Sink, faucet, lights: Standard grade . . . . $ 3,000
Flooring, wall finishes: Laminate/paint . . . . $ 2,000
Construction and installation: Remove wall/increase window/install . . $ 9,500
$35,000

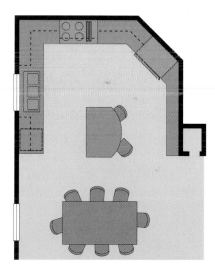

Above: These empty-nesters needed two kinds of seating: cozy dining for just the two of them, and a generous table with lots of seating for when their grown children and grandchildren visit.

One Kitchen, Three Budgets

This outdated kitchen was part of a charming, 100-plus year-old house that would become heart-of-the-home to a professional chef/culinary writer, her husband, and five children between them. The kitchen's cut-up floor plan was hardly up to the new demands. The homeowners ideally wanted to boost the efficiency of their kitchen with more counter space, more cabinet space, an entry closet to minimize clutter at the back door, more daylight, and a suite of up-to-date appliances—including a commercial range, a bigger refrigerator, a more efficient dishwasher, and a built-in microwave. They also wanted to include a baking area and breakfast table.

Their kitchen designer presented them with three options: a plan that effected minimal change, which was the least costly of the three; moderate change with moderate cost; and a high-end, all-out option they wound up choosing. Here's how the three plans looked:

Minimal remodeling floorplan: This plan proposed an island for dining and gathering space; included more counter space and new efficient cabinetry; removed walls at the back door for a less congested feel; and added a full-sized refrigerator, a built-in microwave, and warming drawers. It did not include a commercial-type range because of the island location, did not add more daylight, and incorporated only minimal gathering space.

Moderate remodeling floorplan: This plan proposed removing all of the interior walls and adding a new window. It also added a vegetable sink and warming drawers to the island, a dining table, more daylight, and a 36-inch commercial-style range with hood—plus all of the improvements proposed in the minimal remodeling plan.

All-out remodeling floorplan: The plan that actually materialized turned the kitchen on its side, reshaping it from 12½×17½ feet to 19×13 feet. A butler's pantry was converted into a mudroom with a closet for a more convenient back entry. Alongside the new mudroom was added a 14×16-foot breakfast/family room, with a peninsula dividing it from the kitchen work space. More than double its original size, the revamped, multipurpose kitchen incorporated everything the homeowners wanted—and more.

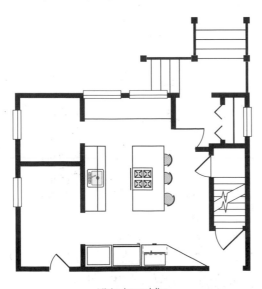

Minimal remodeling

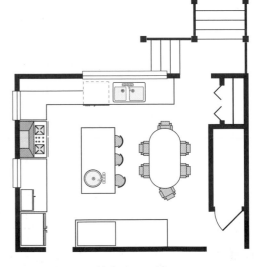

Moderate remodeling

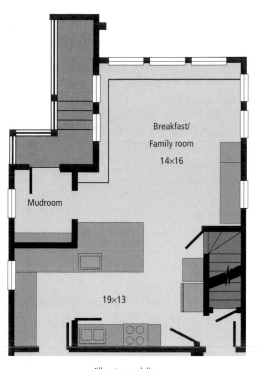

Breakfast/
Family room
14×16

Mudroom

19×13

All-out remodeling

Above: State-of-the-art appliances, including a 36-inch commercial range, were priorities for the chef and culinary writer who renovated and added on to this kitchen.

Left: A granite-top peninsula bisects the renovated kitchen into work space and the new family/breakfast room addition, replete with old-style bookcases that just miss the ceiling. The peninsula houses the sink and establishes an efficient work triangle. The commercial range is on the opposite wall; the refrigerator is to the side.

Special Interests

Though everyone needs a place to prepare meals and eat, the specific needs of families with children are very different from those of people without children at home or serious cooks and entertainers. Consider the following.

Different needs, different solutions

Couple #1 (represented by the floor plan below) is comprised of a husband and wife in their early 30s with three children, ages 2, 4, and 7. They are a on a limited budget. The wife loves to bake cookies, garden, and takes care of the family business. They have an affinity for antiques.

Theirs will be primarily a one-cook kitchen, with room at the island for other activities. They want a traditional cabinet to go with their antiques, maybe maple with a honey-colored stain. (A light stain on a hard-grain wood is the most forgiving when hit with tricycles and such.) Accessories should include a fold-out pantry, trash cans for recycling, tray storage for cookie sheets, and

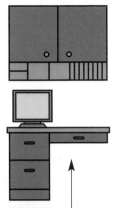

Below and Opposite: **Two floor plans show how the needs of a family with young children were met,** *left,* **and how a couple in their 40s who love to cook gourmet meals were addressed in the same kitchen space.**

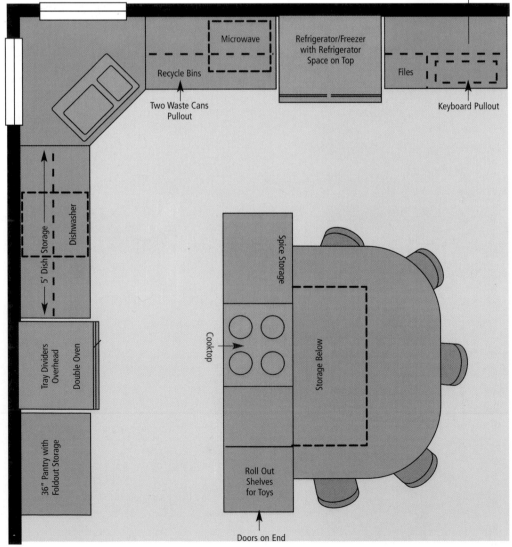

file drawers at the desk.

The appliances should be good quality but not top-of-the-line gourmet equipment. They need a convection oven, a good-size freezer for garden produce, a compost chute, and a sink with double bowls. The countertops can be laminate, and the floor needs to be more durable than wood but more forgiving than tile, for the comfort and safety of the children—probably a laminate also.

Couple #2 (represented by the floor plan below) is a couple in their 40s. They have a dog they love like a child. They entertain friends often and love cooking and eating elaborate gourmet meals paired with good wine.

They are both serious cooks, and so need two distinct work triangles that won't interfere with each other. They would like some dining area in the kitchen for themselves but have a beautiful dining room elsewhere for use when they entertain.

The floor plans show in detail how each couple's needs were met.

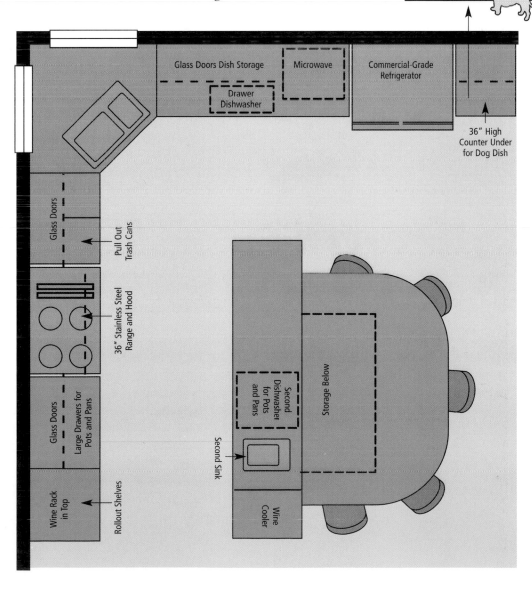

Glass Doors Dish Storage

Microwave

Commercial-Grade Refrigerator

Drawer Dishwasher

36" High Counter Under for Dog Dish

Glass Doors

Pull Out Trash Cans

36" Stainless Steel Range and Hood

Glass Doors

Large Drawers for Pots and Pans

Wine Rack in Top

Rollout Shelves

Second Sink

Second Dishwasher for Pots and Pans

Storage Below

Wine Cooler

Left: A high countertop divides the cooking and cleanup work centers in this gourmet kitchen from the open dining area but allows the cook full view of what's happening at the table.

Calculating Costs

Brace yourself. When it comes to remodeling your kitchen, you'll inevitably part with more money than you expect to spend. Balancing your dreams with financial realities is a complex game of give-and-take, one that demands research and creativity to master. But if you plan wisely and take a few tips from the pros, your next kitchen will not only be a good investment, it will pay off in ways you never expected.

How much should you spend?

Real estate agents agree that you can invest 10 to 15 percent of your home's total value in a kitchen remodeling and expect to recoup a significant portion when you sell the house—anywhere from 50 to 120 percent. In the hottest housing markets, the accepted ratio of the kitchen's remodeling to a home's overall value can climb as high as 25 percent for some homes.

The only way to assess the value of your own investment is to match your precise plans and budgets with local market conditions. If you own a $150,000 house with chipped laminate counters and invest $12,000 in a six-burner professional-style range but little else, you won't see much of a return. Talk to real estate agents who understand local values, tastes, and trends—not just in your area, but also in your own neighborhood specifically.

You should research financing options too. Unlike a loan for a $35,000 car, the interest on a home equity loan is tax deductible. In a competitive lending market, you might turn around and refinance your entire mortgage when the work is done. Considering that a new car declines in value the moment you leave the lot, and a new kitchen holds its value much longer, the investment potential is clear.

What could you spend?

Most of us understand it's possible to spend $100,000 on a kitchen, yet we still imagine luxuries at $25,000. That simply may not be realistic. According to the National Kitchen and Bath Association, the average professionally designed American kitchen remodeling project in 1998 had a price tag of nearly $27,000, including management and labor costs. Most of those kitchens were at least 11×14 feet, and cabinets accounted for roughly half of the total expense. But very few included such high-ticket items as granite or solid-surfacing countertops and large, commercial-style appliances.

To put costs into perspective, we've identified three general categories of remodeling and what you can expect to

Below: Items such as the specialty lighting and windows in this Arts and Crafts-style kitchen look lovely but do drive up the costs of remodeling.

Left: If you've got your heart set on a particular element for your new kitchen—a commercial-style range or a hand-painted tile backsplash, for instance—and you don't have a bottomless purse, budget for those priorities and cut back on items that are less important to you.

achieve in each price range. Figures assume that you're not choosing rock-bottom materials, because you want the kitchen to last more than a year or two.

Modest project ($5,000 to $15,000)

In this price range, you'll typically stay within the existing walls and make no significant changes to the layout. At the low end, you can paint or refurbish existing wood cabinets and replace most of the surfaces and fixtures (e.g., the sink and faucet and a light or two) with no-frills options. You also can swap out some appliances with economically priced models if you keep them in the same position so that no changes in wiring are necessary.

At the high end, you can choose better appliances and replace cabinets (but don't expect any custom sizes or finishes). To get quality in one area, you should be prepared to make sacrifices in another—such as settling for laminate flooring or resilient flooring, forgetting about that snazzy cooktop, and doing some of the work yourself if you have the skills.

In any case, achieving good results with a modest budget depends largely on your ability to research and plan extensively. Expect to endure a lot more inconvenience than a homeowner who pays a seasoned professional to manage all the details.

Midrange project ($15,000 to $30,000)

Even at $15,000, you can expect good-quality stock cabinets. Let the budget grow and you can opt for laminate counters with stylish edging and an entirely new suite of midrange appliances. Moreover, you can make some improvements to the layout—perhaps even opening the existing space to another room.

Beware, however, of potential budget-busters that lurk in any wall you plan to remove. The extra demolition, carpentry, and finishing work alone can easily add $1,000, even in a wall that isn't load-bearing. And the total cost may be many times higher. What kind of surface damage to surrounding spaces will your remodeling cause? And what's inside those walls you're opening? Will you have to reroute plumbing, ducts, or electrical cables? Are the floors uneven between spaces, demanding an entirely new floor throughout? Will you need a specially engineered beam to support a load-bearing span? Those are the possible perils of just opening up the space. If you're planning on expanding the kitchen into an adjacent area, you're likely to spend substantially more.

In its *2000/2001 Cost vs. Value* study, the trade magazine *Remodeling* pegged the average "major kitchen remodeling" at just

below $31,000 (including contractor costs determined by R.S. Means, a leading publisher of national construction costs). For that price, a kitchen roughly 12×16 feet, acquired an improved layout with a 3×5-foot island, new semicustom cabinets (30 linear feet), new appliances (with a separate wall oven and cooktop), custom lighting, and nice laminate counters and resilient flooring. For many potential remodelers, that cost sounds prohibitive. But there's good news in the report, too: The average amount recouped through increased resale values ranged from 67 percent in the West to 77 percent in the East. And in hot spots like Philadelphia and Minneapolis, the return on investment climbed to 98 percent or higher. (Visit www.remodeling.hw.net for more information.)

CUTTING COSTS

If you're having trouble squaring your dreams with your bank account, there are things you can do to bring your budget in line. Obviously, you can change the scope of your project—doing less construction work and eliminating luxury materials. But the following tips, combining hard work with creativity, can help you keep more of your wish list intact.

• Mix and match materials. Reserve expensive countertops for a small island and put in laminate or ceramic tile elsewhere.

• Use furniture creatively to achieve an unfitted look on a budget. Create an island from an old table or a pantry from an armoire.

• Do some of the work yourself. Be your own general contractor and save roughly 10 to 20 percent overall. Just be absolutely sure you're qualified and that you have time to oversee every detail of your remodeling.

• Shop carefully. Contractors and plumbers often cover their costs by charging list prices for materials. If you buy direct, your material costs may be significantly lower. Let those who bid on your projects know which materials you plan to buy.

• Pay for expertise. Hire an architect, kitchen designer, or general contractor. The pros will do the legwork for you and can keep you from making mistakes that cost more than the fees they charge.

• Compromise smart. If you have to choose between expensive materials and expensive labor, choose the labor. A good cabinetmaker, carpenter, or decorative painter can make even mundane materials look like a million.

• Don't overbuy. The difference between "good," "better" and "best" appliances is often in the bells and whistles. Determine your minimum requirements and which extras you're willing to pay for.

Deluxe project ($30,000 and up)

Most designers will tell you that $30,000 or $40,000 will not buy you a truly "deluxe" kitchen. And they're right. That is a serious amount of money, but it takes a very savvy, well-educated consumer—one who's willing to make some compromises and devote significant time to his or her own project—to achieve high-end luxuries for "so little."

A bit of shopping reveals the cold facts. Do you have your heart set on a commercial-style range and fridge? Add the requisite vent hood, and the price tag could easily exceed $15,000 for these appliances alone. Add such amenities as wine chillers, extra ovens, and special drawers to keep veggies crisp and dinner warm and you could be looking at a $30,000 appliance suite. Custom cabinets often command $500 or more per linear foot. So if you have even 30 linear feet of cabinets, that tab also runs at least $15,000. The budget is broken before you even begin to consider such sought-after luxuries as granite-slab countertops ($10,000 for a typical installation) and hardwood floors ($2,000 to $5,000), not to mention design and construction costs.

What will you spend?

Every kitchen job is highly individual. Costs vary depending on the materials you choose as well as on the condition of your home. A homeowner who has old knob-and-tube wiring may end up spending as much as $5,000 to $7,000 just to update the plumbing and electrical systems. The cost of a simple addition runs about $150 per square foot and up.

To estimate costs of your own project as accurately as possible, there's no substitute for a detailed plan. First, sketch the precise layout of your intended kitchen. You'll undoubtedly change things later, but to get a clear picture of costs, you have to start somewhere. Next, list every conceivable item you'll buy and start shopping to estimate prices—fixture by fixture, cabinet by cabinet. (Cabinet prices per foot might be only half your true cost; they're based on a basic box). There's no substitute for actually

visiting local stores and showrooms to narrow your choices and get accurate figures.

After you've burned a little shoe leather, you can start refining your plan. Identify priorities and eliminate luxuries you can live without. This is a good time to consult with a designer and start soliciting bids for work: You have a good idea what things cost, you know what you intend to spend, and you know what you hope to achieve.

One final note: Even the most carefully planned project will have unforeseen costs, which often add 20 percent to a budget. If you don't have that wiggle room, create a simpler plan up front. You'll sleep better at night and still enjoy your new kitchen in the morning.

Left: When setting your remodeling priorities, think about how you use your kitchen and what aspects of it are most pleasing to you. If you have a lovely view, you might want to capitalize on that and enlarge an existing window or install a specialty window such as this one.

Working with a Contractor

When you're planning a remodeling project, it's natural to consider what you want out of the deal. But you must also know what your contractor will need to get the job done well. Your understanding of the planning, preparation, and construction process helps you communicate better and complete a successful project. Explore these ways to help you help your contractor.

Get focused (and be consistent)

Contractors appreciate clients who can clearly communicate their vision. Collect ideas and images from magazines and books. Present these examples to your contractor, and if you have details you are intent on including, mention them specifically.

Visually communicating ideas puts everyone on the same page. Pictures are especially helpful to your contractor if you don't have the vocabulary to explain the effect or materials you're after.

Below: Even if you plan to do much of the remodeling work yourself, projects such as this birch-motif backsplash are often best done by a professional. That way you won't have yourself to blame if, because of your inexperience, it doesn't turn out quite the way you had expected.

DESIGNER TIP

Try to get bids from two or three contractors for your kitchen project, and get them in writing. Remember that price is not the only consideration; there are the issues of personality, quality workmanship, and professionalism, too. Be sure to ask for references from anyone who gives you a bid—from recent work they've done and five to eight years ago—so you can ask questions about how the work has held up.

Clear communication also translates into fewer surprises once work is under way. Changed orders or reconsidered decisions are a part of every remodeling effort, but they eat your money and your contractor's time, and the latter might already be earmarked for the next client's project.

Be realistic about your budget

When planning with your contractor, be honest about your budget. If a few items push you over the top, it's likely your contractor can help you get the look you want for less by suggesting some alternative materials. Keep in mind, though, that price tags at the local home center may be lower than those quoted by your contractor. Sometimes this is due to standard markups on materials, but estimates may also reflect handling requirements and installation costs.

Mind your money matters

The contract you sign will stipulate when payments are due. Plan to adhere to these dates without exception. You must have your financial ducks in a row before you start a project. Late payments will undoubtedly slow the process, especially if you're working with an independent remodeler who needs those payments to purchase your materials.

Prepare the site; corral the dogs

Whether your kitchen project involves minor or major structural modification, remove any obstacles to site access. Some contractors will move large items such as furniture without charge; others won't. Discuss your contractor's policy in advance to prevent surprises. Remove all items of value (dishes, pictures, vases, etc.) from the space. Don't let pets get underfoot, and don't

Left: A general contractor can do most jobs. If there's an aspect of your kitchen plan that requires a special skill—such as the finish carpentry it took to create this post-and-beam kitchen—you or your contractor will likely have call in a craftsperson with the expertise you need.

make workers responsible for preventing their escape through a doorway or a wall opening. They've got enough to do.

Expect chaos

Remodeling is a messy business. Yet some homeowners are still surprised by the amount of dust and upheaval it generates. Even with the best of circumstances, there's a good chance it's going to be stressful. Discuss these and other peacekeeping issues beforehand, including rules about smoking in the house, which bathroom to use, where to park vehicles, and so on. Also, avoid the work zone as much as possible, for your safety and that of the workers. Keep in mind that children are notorious for their fascination with the tools and big messes of remodeling. Arrange a few supervised visits to satisfy their curiosity, but make sure they are otherwise occupied and out of harm's way.

Of course every project will involve different details, but observing these fundamental guidelines will promote mutual goodwill between you and your contractor. As in most business relationhips,

COPING WITH A KITCHEN OVERHAUL

From the time you contract with your builder, discussions should include strategies for minimizing disruption to your home, family, and lifestyle. Some contractors will not start a project until everything on order has arrived; the old cabinets will not be removed, for example, until the new ones are in the warehouse. Careful timing of orders can save the family unnecessary discomfort. Here are a few more strategies for surviving the chaos of a kitchen remodel.

• Set up a temporary kitchen—a microwave oven, countertop, and sink—in the basement, laundry room, or extra bathroom.

• Use carpet runners and plastic partitions called dust curtains to minimize the impact of grime. Ask about limiting worker access into the home to one entrance.

• Outline your menus. Ask your contractor how long you'll be without the use of a kitchen and plan accordingly. Remember that restaurant coupon book you bought last spring? Use it.

• Have a backup plan. Talk to friends and relatives and arrange an exchange of services: You bring the groceries, and everyone helps prepare a meal in their kitchen.

• Don't internalize stress: Picture yourself as a good person in a tough situation. Know your stress buttons and work to balance the tension when it becomes too much for you. Take a walk, go to the gym, or head to the library.

• Monitor your self-image: You know all of those TV commercials showing happy people living in spotless homes? Forget about them. Your home's condition during a remodeling project is not a reflection of your worth.

attitude can make all the difference. A contractor who sees that you respect his time and services is likely to reciprocate by respecting you and your home and delivering the quality you expect.

Your Final Design Checklist

Spare yourself some hassle and headache by checking your new kitchen's final design against this checklist of frequently overlooked points before ordering or work begins.

■ Is there plenty of counter space between appliances and sinks?

■ Is there enough space in kitchen corners to open drawers and doors fully?

■ Have you planned adjustable, roll-out, and vertical storage for the cabinets?

■ Do the cabinets come with handles or with pulls?

■ Where will the pulls be placed on the cabinets? Will their design interfere with nearby appliance, door, or drawer openings?

■ Is the microwave at the right height for pulling out hot items? Can children use it safely?

■ Have you planned sufficient undercabinet lighting?

■ Are light fixtures planned for above the sink, cooktop, or range?

■ Has the location of switch controls for lighting been planned?

Right: One of the first—and most important—questions you can ask about your kitchen plan is whether you will have enough storage space. There is no shortage of it in this kitchen, where base and wall cabinets cover nearly every inch.

DESIGNER TIP

Make certain that your appliances and cabinetry will fit together before you order either. For each appliance that you'll be using, get the manufacturer's specifications and check them against your cabinet specifications.

Always double-check manufacturer's specifications for appliances. For instance, heights for appliance drawers for warming, refrigeration, and dishwashing will vary by manufacturer.

■ Has the toe kick below the cabinets been designed for the thickness of your flooring?
■ Will the new kitchen floor match the style and height of flooring in adjoining rooms? How will it be joined?
■ Will new walls be trimmed with baseboard or molding at the floor?
■ Will this baseboard or cove meet the molding around the doors?
■ How will the walls be finished? Will they have to be prepared for painting or wallpaper?
■ How will the wall and ceiling finishes meet?
■ Do you have plenty of electrical outlets? If you're planning an island or peninsula, don't forget outlets there, too.

Double-check your plan

■ Is the work-flow uninterrupted?

Traffic should flow around the kitchen's work triangle(s)—not through it. Likewise, special zones such as coffee/juice zones and snack centers shouldn't cross the work triangle. Otherwise collisions between the cook(s) and anyone passing through are likely. Such crossings are annoying at best, extremely dangerous at worst.

■ Is there space between work centers and zones?

It's best to allow 4 to 6 feet between the sink and the range, 4 to 7 feet between the refrigerator and sink, and 4 to 9 feet between the range and refrigerator. Total space between all three points on the triangle should add up to no more than 26 feet. More than this standard can make kitchen work inefficient and tiring. Remember, too, that for all but zealous baking enthusiasts, ovens can be placed outside the work triangle.

■ Is there counter space near each work center or zone?

Counter space on both sides of the sink, 18 to 24 inches, is a must. You also need space near the refrigerator—at least 15 inches on the handle side—to set food going in or out. Similarly essential is a heat-resistant 15- to 18-inch space on both sides of a cooktop and on one side of a wall-mounted oven for hot pans and supplies.

■ Do you have enough storage space where you need it?

Basic storage standards suggest 18 square feet of cabinet space plus an additional half a square foot for each family member. Plan storage space where the item will be used first: pot storage near the range and food storage near the main prep area. You'll need cool storage, too: 12 cubic feet of refrigerator-freezer combo for two people, plus 2 cubic feet for each additional family member. Remember, too, that you needn't store everything within an arm's reach. Infrequently used equipment and specialty tools can be stored in a pantry closet near the kitchen center.

■ Last but not least, will you enjoy your kitchen?

Whether you're reviving your kitchen or giving it a to-the-studs makeover, the time and money that you put into the project should result in a space that you enjoy immensely. Just think of the time spent in your kitchen every day. So if you're excited about your plans, forge ahead. But if parts of your kitchen plan nag at you, go back and review them, looking for alternatives and other solutions. If you've done the planning yourself, get a pro's opinion; if you've been working with someone, seek another opinion. A kitchen you love is what you're after!

Above: **On a final run-through of the details of your kitchen plan, consider if you've placed dangerous items such as the knife drawer in a place that may be convenient for you but too accessible for small children.**

Right: Wood floors in a kitchen require almost-daily sweeping or vacuuming and frequent washes with warm water and an oil soap (or a soap specially formulated for wood floors). Be sure to wipe up any spills immediately.

The Easy-Clean Kitchen

Visions of high style, not low maintenance, drive kitchen projects. However, unless you plan to make your newly remodeled kitchen purely for show and not for dough (the kind you roll out), let's be realistic: It's going to get dirty. To minimize the mess potential, consider some features at the design stage that will prevent your dream kitchen from becoming a cleaning nightmare.

A tight triangle

A good work triangle—arrangement of the cooktop, sink, and refrigerator—minimizes the distance you have to carry things in the kitchen. It's the carrying that often leads to spills and messy pile-ups. One architect calls the area between workstations "drip space," so she puts the cooktop and sink close together to minimize messes. A center island can often compensate for a poor work triangle. If your kitchen is too small for a permanent island, a rolling cart or table can serve the same purpose.

Flowing floors

Thanks to gravity, most kitchen dirt ends up on the floor. Nothing will save you from regular cleaning, but the fewer the seams or gaps in your floor, the fewer places for dirt to collect. The dirtiest place in any kitchen is the seam between the vertical surface of the toe-kick and the horizontal surface of the floor. That can be eliminated by "rolling" the edge of the floor up to the toe-kick, replacing the right-angle joint with a smooth curve. The technique is easiest with vinyl, linoleum, and tile, but it's also possible with wood if you have the edge pieces custom-milled.

Ceramic tile flooring is beautiful, but needs constant attention. It obligates you to a daily sweeping. To make tile look cleaner, use large squares with narrow grout lines.

When you do have to clean the kitchen floor, technology can make the job easier. Consider a central vacuum system with an automatic dustpan inlet that installs in the baseboard or cabinetry toe-kick. You simply sweep dirt from the floor into the opening, and it gets sucked into a vacuum bag.

Full enclosure

Handy receptacles for kitchen trash ease cleanup. Food scraps can go down the disposal, but you need a hidden place for food packaging as well. If you live in a community with a recycling program, use different containers to sort paper, plastic, cardboard, and glass from nonrecyclable items. Sort as you work in the kitchen, and you'll save a step on trash day.

In addition to your trash, put away your treasures. Open shelves provide flexible storage, but they do gather dust easily. Full or partial glass doors or display cases can block out much of the dust without blocking views of what's inside. But keep in mind that this creates a different cleaning chore: You have to clean the glass.

Grime-fighting cabinets

Cabinets that have flat doors with a baked-on finish are easiest to clean. Painted cabinets with a high-gloss finish show dirt, but they're easiest to wipe down. Stained cabinets with a flatter, or no-gloss finish, don't show dirt as much, but they're more easily marred and harder to touch up. Raised-panel doors and elaborate molding around cabinetry look nice, but they are harder to clean. The more elaborate the molding, the greater the impact on maintenance.

Some drawers have acrylic utensil liners that can be thrown right into the dishwasher.

When your fingers are greasy, pulls and handles keep the mess off the cabinetry surface, unlike doors and drawers you have to reach a hand under to open. Look for hardware that makes it easy to open doors and drawers or you'll swap cleaning doors for cleaning handles. Three-inch-long metal pulls work nicely because you can open the door or drawer with one finger.

Counter-sink connection

How your sink is attached to the countertop affects ease of cleaning. Undermount sinks, attached to the underside of the countertop, make it easy to wipe messes from the counter right into the sink. Self-rimming sinks, on the other hand, have a perimeter lip that's sealed with a bead of caulk and can be a dirt collector. Perhaps the best solution is an integral sink in which the bowl and surrounding counter are one large piece of the same material, typically solid-surfacing or stainless steel. The lack of seams between the sink and countertop means there's nowhere for dirt to collect.

If an integral sink is too expensive, there's a cheaper solution: Go out and buy a cutting board. Put the board over the countertop, then slid cuttings right into the sink.

The area behind the sink can be a

COUNTERTOP CONTAINMENT

Generally, the smoother the surface of your countertop and the fewer the seams, nooks, and crannies, the better. Curving your countertop up the wall creates a seamless backsplash that eliminates the dirt-catching right-angle joint where the counter meets the wall. In front, make sure the countertop edge overhangs the cabinet doors or drawers somewhat. Otherwise spills may get into cabinets or seep into drawers.

trouble spot, too. Most configurations leave about a 1-inch gap between the back edge of the sink and the backsplash. It's a space just wide enough to attract dirt but too narrow to clean easily. You can solve the problem by making the sink countertop 1½ inches deeper. The extra depth is made possible with 2×4s placed between standard 24-inch-deep base cabinets and the wall. With the counter at 25½ inches deep, there's just enough extra space behind the sink that it can be easily wiped with a sponge or rag.

Able appliances

Self-cleaning ovens, frost-free freezers, refrigerators with spill-catching shelves, and dishwashers with a range of cycles all help cut down on kitchen cleanup chores. If you've ever had to clean dirty drip pans from a stove top with conventional burners, you'll appreciate cooktops with smooth, ceramic surfaces. Even sealed gas burners with grates over the top are a cinch to clean.

Grease and smoke from cooking are common culprits in dirty kitchens, but a properly sized exhaust fan can help reduce greasy buildup on surfaces.

Built-in appliances eliminate common dirt traps, such as the space behind the refrigerator or gaps between a freestanding range and the adjacent countertops.

Left: **Stainless steel is a favored material in many kitchens—for sinks, appliances, and countertops—because it wipes up easily with warm water and soap and doesn't (considering its name) stain.**

Index